LIVING IN SOUTH AFRICA

What It Takes

MARTIN LEIGH

About the Front Cover

The front cover features a photograph taken by the author in the Lesotho Highlands, often called the "Mountain Kingdom." This region, known for its dramatic peaks and high-altitude plateaus, forms part of the landscape along the border between South Africa and Lesotho. The image reflects the rural character and natural beauty of the area, which plays an important role in the daily life and geography of the region.

LIVING IN SOUTH AFRICA:

What it Takes

By

Martin Leigh

Published by CIEL GLOBAL
https://www.cielglobal.world

Foreword/Author's Note — Martin Leigh

Beyond the Headlines:
Unveiling the True South Africa

For more than **four decades**, I have had the profound privilege of calling **South Africa** my home. I've walked its mountains, crossed its vast plains, navigated its vibrant cities, and, most importantly, shared life with its incredibly diverse people. Yet, in my conversations with friends and strangers across the globe, I've come to a disappointing realization: for many, this stunning, complex, and beautiful land remains little more than a collection of headlines—a place often misunderstood, frequently feared, and rarely truly known.

It is a genuine **shame** that a nation bursting with such natural splendor, human warmth, and compelling history is so often dismissed by a single, isolating word: **"dangerous."** I speak to countless individuals who hold a mental image shaped primarily by decades-old news stories or generalized anxieties, leading them to believe this extraordinary destination is simply too risky to visit. They imagine a place perpetually on edge, missing the dynamic, resilient, and welcoming reality that countless residents and tourists experience every single day.

This book is my attempt to bridge that gap—to take you **beyond the gate and the guard** and into the heart of the country I know and love. We will journey through South Africa's breathtaking landscapes, from the iconic Table Mountain to the wild expanse of the Kruger National Park. Crucially, we will also embark on a deeper, more challenging, but ultimately essential exploration of its **complex history**. We cannot truly appreciate the present without understanding the powerful currents of colonialism, the oppressive system of **Apartheid**, and the miraculous, often difficult, birth of the "Rainbow Nation." And then finally to the current Government and their challenges ahead.

This is not a travel guide focused only on luxury hotels; it is an invitation to **understand**. It is my hope that by sharing the stories, the struggles, and the soaring beauty of this unique place, I can challenge the misconceptions that keep so many away. South Africa is a land of contrasts, yes, but it is also a land of profound **hope, resilience, and unparalleled hospitality**. Prepare to look closer, to understand its depths, and perhaps, to fall in love with the true South Africa, just as I did so many years ago.

COPYRIGHT

Living in South Africa – What It Takes
Copyright © 2025 by **Martin Leigh**
All rights reserved.

Photographs
All photographs in this book are © **Martin Leigh**, except where otherwise attributed.

This book is intended for informational and educational purposes only. The author and publisher disclaim all liability arising directly or indirectly from the application or use of the information contained herein. Readers should consult appropriate professionals for advice tailored to their individual circumstances.

ISBN: 979-8-9957221-2-0

ABOUT THE AUTHOR

Martin Leigh

Born and raised in Johannesburg, South Africa, Martin spent more than forty years immersed in the country that shaped his outlook and identity. After living in the United Kingdom for six years and Thailand for over fifteen, South Africa remains deeply rooted in his heart.

A graduate of the University of the Witwatersrand (Wits), Martin witnessed South Africa's historic transformation during the first democratic elections in 1994. Having seen, breathed, and lived the nation's journey toward full democracy, he brings a unique personal perspective to his writing.

Martin has travelled widely across southern Africa — including Lesotho, Swaziland, Zimbabwe, Zambia, Mozambique, Namibia, and Botswana — gaining an appreciation for the region's breadth and spirit. His teaching career in Thailand, where he has spent the past fifteen years instructing Math, Physics, Chemistry, Biology, and English to Thai, Korean, and Chinese students, has further broadened his worldview.

He continues to travel regularly between South Africa, the UK, and Asia, drawing inspiration from the contrasts and connections among these regions. Through his work, Martin hopes to offer readers a grounded, nuanced portrait of South Africa — one that acknowledges its challenges while celebrating its beauty, resilience, and promise.

ACKNOWLEDGMENTS

Writing a book is often a solitary act, but completing it is invariably a collaborative effort. It is an immense privilege to thank the many people and institutions who made this work possible.

This book owes its existence first and foremost to my publishing team. I extend my profound gratitude to my editor, **Eugenia Canaan**, whose insightful critique and unwavering belief in this project transformed a rough manuscript into a cohesive narrative. Her sharp eye and intellectual partnership were invaluable.

Illustrative representation of South Africa's vibrant cultural diversity.

TABLE OF CONTENTS

Chapter 1 — Understanding South Africa

South Africa is a country that defies simple descriptions. It is a land of extraordinary beauty — wide open spaces, dramatic coastlines, and a cultural richness found in few places on earth — and at the same time a nation shaped by a complex, often difficult history.

To understand South Africa is to look closely at both sides of this reality: the resilience of its people, and the challenges woven into everyday life. This chapter offers the foundations needed to see the country as it truly is, beyond headlines and assumptions.

1. Understanding South Africa

South Africa is a country of immense diversity, complexity, and striking beauty, often referred to as the **"Rainbow Nation."** To understand it, we should focus on its geography, history, economy, and culture.

Key Facts and Geography

- **Capital Cities:** South Africa has three capital cities: **Pretoria** (Administrative), **Cape Town** (Legislative), and **Bloemfontein** (Judicial). The biggest city is **Johannesburg**. Collectively with Pretoria (now called Tshwane) and Vereeniging (Vaal Triangle) is called Gauteng. (Place of gold).
- **Population & Languages:** It has a highly diverse population of over 60 million people and **12 official languages** (including English, Zulu, Xhosa, Afrikaans, and Sotho), reflecting its cultural mosaic.
- **Geography:** Known for its dramatic landscapes, from the iconic **Table Mountain** in Cape Town to the vast central **Highveld** plateau and the sub-tropical coastlines of KwaZulu-Natal.

History: From Apartheid to Democracy

The history of South Africa is dominated by the system of Apartheid (Afrikaans for "apartness"), which enforced racial segregation and political/economic discrimination against non-white groups from 1948 until 1994.

- **Resistance**: Figures like Nelson Mandela and the African National Congress (ANC) led decades of resistance, resulting in Mandela's 27 years of imprisonment.

- **1994 Election**: The country transitioned to democracy with the first non-racial democratic election in 1994, marking the official end of Apartheid and ushering in reconciliation under President Mandela.

- **Current Challenges:** Despite the democratic transition, the nation still grapples with the historical legacies of deep economic inequality and persistent high unemployment.

Economy and Resources

South Africa is the most industrialized economy in Africa, but it faces significant infrastructure challenges.

- **Natural Resources**: It is extremely rich in natural resources, being a global leader in the production of platinum, gold, diamonds, and chromium.

- **Key Sectors**: The economy is driven by mining, manufacturing, finance, and tourism.

- **Load Shedding**: A major contemporary issue is "load shedding" (planned, rolling electricity blackouts) due to chronic infrastructure problems at the state-owned power utility, Eskom.

Culture and Tourism

- **Cuisine**: South African cuisine is a blend of indigenous, Dutch, Indian, and Malaysian influences. You must try braai (barbecue), biltong (dried cured meat), and bobotie (a sweet, curried mince dish with an egg topping).

- **Wildlife**: It is one of the world's premier destinations for ecotourism, particularly known for its "Big Five" viewing opportunities (lion, leopard, rhino, elephant, and buffalo) in parks like the Kruger National Park.

- **Vibrant Arts**: The country has a thriving music, art, and film scene, heavily influenced by its socio-political history.

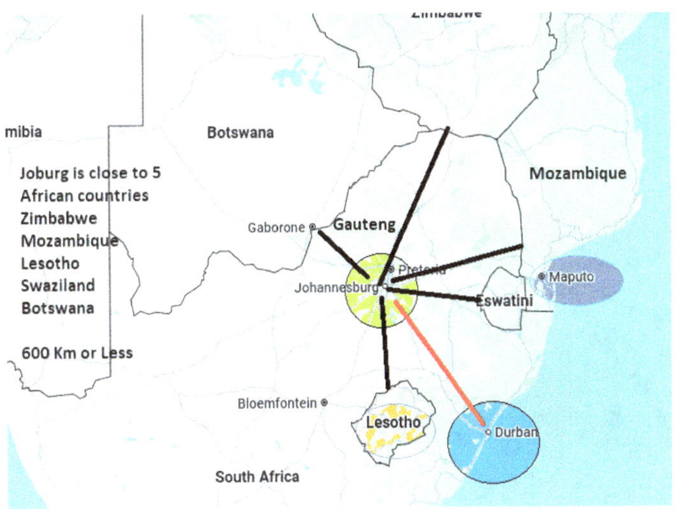

Chapter 2 — Johannesburg

Johannesburg is a city that grew out of urgency — born almost overnight from the discovery of gold and shaped by the ambitions, conflicts, and hopes of millions who came seeking a new life. It is not an easy city, nor a simple one, but it is undeniably the engine that drives much of South Africa's economy and identity.

To understand modern South Africa, you must first understand Johannesburg: its energy, its contradictions, and its central role in the country's past and present.

2. Johannesburg

The history of Johannesburg, often called "eGoli" (the place of gold), is a dramatic story defined almost entirely by the discovery of gold, rapid urbanization, and its central role in South Africa's economic and political evolution.

The Gold Rush and Founding (1886)

- **Discovery**: The city's history begins abruptly in 1886 with the discovery of vast, rich gold deposits along the Witwatersrand (White Water Ridge), then part of the South African Republic (ZAR). The discovery was primarily attributed to an Australian prospector, George Harrison.

- **Rapid Birth**: A massive gold rush ensued, attracting prospectors, miners, and fortune-seekers from all over the world. A makeshift tent town quickly sprang up near the main reef.

- **Official Foundation**: The settlement was officially proclaimed a public gold field in September 1886. The town was likely named after two officials involved in surveying the area, both named Johannes (Johannes Rissik and Christiaan Johannes Joubert). Johannesburg lacked the careful planning of other cities and grew chaotically based on the mining camp structure.

Early Development and Conflict (Late 19th Century)

- **"Uitlanders" and Tensions**: The influx of thousands of foreign miners and businessmen (known as Uitlanders—"outlanders") created severe political tension with the conservative ZAR government, led by Paul Kruger. The Uitlanders, though wealthy and numerous, were denied voting rights.

- **Boer Wars**: These tensions ultimately contributed to the outbreak of the Second Anglo-Boer War (1899–1902). After the British won the war, the Transvaal (which included Johannesburg) became a British colony.

- **Industrialization:** Under British control, the deep-level gold mining industry was formalized and industrialized, driving massive economic growth but also establishing the foundation for segregationist labor practices.

Segregation and Apartheid (20th Century)

- **Influx Control**: As the city grew, the authorities implemented laws to control the movement and residence of Black African populations, restricting them to specific townships (like Soweto—South Western Townships) situated outside the white city center.

- **Economic Engine**: Throughout the 20th century, Johannesburg cemented its role as the financial and economic hub of Southern Africa, largely due to the gold industry, which provided the capital for banks and corporations.

- **Anti-Apartheid Struggle**: Johannesburg and its surrounding townships were central to the resistance movement against the Apartheid regime. Key events include the Sharpeville Massacre (1960) and the Soweto Uprising (1976), which were defining moments in the struggle for democracy.

The Modern Era (Post-1994)

- **Democratic Transition**: Following the end of Apartheid and the 1994 democratic election, Johannesburg became the capital of the newly formed Gauteng province (the economic powerhouse of South Africa).

- **Inner City Challenges**: The city center experienced a period of urban decay as businesses and many residents moved to northern suburbs (like Sandton). This led to challenges related to crime, poverty, and abandoned buildings.

- **Revitalization**: In recent years, massive efforts have been made toward inner-city revitalization and regeneration, particularly in areas like Maboneng and Braamfontein.

- **Current Role**: Today, Johannesburg is a dynamic, sprawling metropolis—the financial heart of Africa—still struggling with the complex historical legacies of inequality and urban management, but pulsing with diverse energy and culture.

Johannesburg, being South Africa's largest city and economic hub, is close to several African countries.

- While the city itself is not *right* on a border, it is in the province of Gauteng, which is centrally located relative to South Africa's surrounding neighbours.

- South Africa is bordered by a total of five independent countries, plus one country that is completely surrounded by South African territory.

- The Closest African Countries to Johannesburg:

Country	Proximity to Johannesburg	Border Status with South Africa
1. Lesotho	Closest. It is entirely surrounded by South African territory (an enclave). The border is easily reached via a short drive from Johannesburg.	Enclave (Fully surrounded)
2. Eswatini (formerly Swaziland)	Very Close. Located to the east/northeast of Gauteng.	Shares a border with South Africa
3. Mozambique	Close. Located to the east/northeast, accessible via the Mpumalanga province.	Shares a border with South Africa
4. Botswana	Close. Located to the northwest of Gauteng. Gaborone, Botswana's capital, is a relatively short drive away.	Shares a border with South Africa
5. Zimbabwe	Close. Located to the north, accessible via the Limpopo province.	Shares a border with South Africa
6. Namibia	Further. Located to the west/northwest of South Africa. While bordering the country, it's the furthest from Johannesburg's immediate area.	Shares a border with South Africa

- So, if you count the countries that share a boundary with South Africa, the number is six in total (Namibia, Botswana, Zimbabwe, Mozambique, Eswatini, and Lesotho).

- The countries that are the most easily accessible by road from Johannesburg are Lesotho, Eswatini, and Botswana.

Johannesburg is often the gateway for overland travel to Southern Africa. Here are the approximate **driving distances** and **travel times** from Johannesburg to the capital cities of its closest neighbouring countries:

Neighboring Country	Capital City	Approximate Driving Distance (km)	Approximate Driving Time (Hours)
Botswana	Gaborone	335 km	4.5 - 6 hours
Eswatini (Swaziland)	Mbabane	362 km	4.5 - 5 hours
Lesotho	Maseru	418 km	5 - 6 hours
Mozambique	Maputo	541 km	6 - 7 hours
Zimbabwe	Harare	1,113 km	12 - 14 hours
Namibia	Windhoek	~1,500 km	17 - 19 hours

IMPORTANT TRAVEL NOTES

- **Border Crossings:** The driving times listed above are for the actual road travel and **do not include time spent at border control**. Border crossings can add significant time, ranging from 30 minutes to several hours, especially during peak seasons (holidays, weekends).

- **Lesotho (Enclave):** Maseru is the furthest of the three most accessible capitals, but the country is completely surrounded by South Africa.

- **Zimbabwe:** The long drive to Harare involves crossing the Beitbridge border, which is known for having long wait times. Many travelers prefer to fly this route.

- **Mozambique:** The drive to Maputo is straightforward via the N4 highway, but the border crossing to Maputo is a factor.

Cradle of Humankind – April, 2025

A UNESCO World Heritage Site located northwest of Johannesburg, the Cradle of Humankind is one of the world's richest hominid fossil areas and a major landmark of the greater Gauteng region.

Chapter 3 — Soweto

Soweto is far more than the place so many people have heard about in news headlines. It is a living community — vibrant, creative, and deeply rooted in the struggle for freedom. Born out of forced segregation but transformed by courage and resilience, Soweto became the heartbeat of resistance during the apartheid years and remains a symbol of South Africa's determination to move forward.

To understand the country's story, you must listen to the voices that rose from these streets, and the spirit that continues to shape them today.

3. Soweto

Soweto is one of the most historically and politically significant urban areas in South Africa. It is a vast, sprawling metropolitan area southwest of Johannesburg that was born out of, and became the epicenter of resistance against, the Apartheid system.

The name **Soweto** is an acronym for **South Western Townships**.

History and Creation

- **Forced Segregation:** Soweto was not a natural city but a cluster of townships created by the white minority government starting in the 1930s. Its primary purpose was to house the Black African workforce needed for Johannesburg's gold mines and industries, while keeping them separated from the white city center by a buffer zone (a railway line, river, or industrial area).

- **Rapid, Unplanned Growth:** As the government systematically cleared "Black Spots" (Black neighborhoods in white areas, like Sophiatown) and forcibly relocated residents, Soweto grew rapidly and chaotically. The housing provided, primarily the monotonous "matchbox houses," was basic and lacked essential services like electricity and plumbing for decades.

- **Melting Pot:** Despite the hardships, Soweto became a vibrant melting pot of different Black South African ethnic groups (Zulu, Xhosa, Sotho, etc.), forging a unique, cosmopolitan urban culture distinct from rural life.

Center of the Anti-Apartheid Struggle

Soweto's political significance is immense; it was the focal point for major resistance against the oppressive government.

- **The Freedom Charter (1955):** The foundational document of the struggle for a non-racial South Africa was adopted in **Kliptown, Soweto**, at the Congress of the People. I am not sure how many promises the ANC has kept, but it is a kind of wish list – if only.

- **The Soweto Uprising (June 16, 1976):** This event is the most critical moment in Soweto's history. It began as a peaceful protest led by Black high school students against the government's mandatory use of **Afrikaans** as a medium of instruction. Police violently suppressed the protest, killing many children. The famous photograph of a dying **Hector Pieterson** became an international symbol of the brutality of Apartheid. The uprising sparked renewed internal and international opposition to the regime.

- **Home of Heroes:** Soweto was the residence of some of the most important anti-Apartheid figures, including **Nelson Mandela** and **Archbishop Desmond Tutu**, whose homes were famously located on the same street, **Vilakazi Street** in Orlando West.

Soweto Today

Since the end of Apartheid in 1994, Soweto has undergone significant development and transformation:

- **Modernization:** It is no longer just a collection of segregated townships but a vital part of the City of Johannesburg. Infrastructure has improved, with better roads, services, and the establishment of massive shopping centers (like Maponya Mall) and sports facilities (like the FNB Stadium/Soccer City).

- **Contrasts:** Soweto remains a place of striking contrasts, with wealthy, modern suburbs existing alongside informal settlements and the original "matchbox" houses, reflecting the enduring economic inequalities inherited from Apartheid.

- **Tourism:** It is a major tourist destination, drawing visitors interested in history and culture. Key sites include:

    - The **Hector Pieterson Memorial and Museum**.

- o The **Mandela House Museum** on Vilakazi Street.

- o The **Orlando Towers** (now a distinctive landmark and extreme sports site).

In essence, Soweto is not just a geographical location; it is a **symbol of survival, resistance, and the triumph of the human spirit** that defines modern South Africa.

The Zulu people continue to preserve their customs while engaging dynamically with modern South African life, maintaining a strong cultural presence within the broader national mosaic.

Mandela's Old House in Soweto

Liliesleaf Farm, Johannesburg — historic underground headquarters of the anti-apartheid struggle and the site of the 1963 Rivonia arrests that led to the Rivonia Trial.

Liliesleaf Farm, Johannesburg — historic meeting place of anti-apartheid leaders.

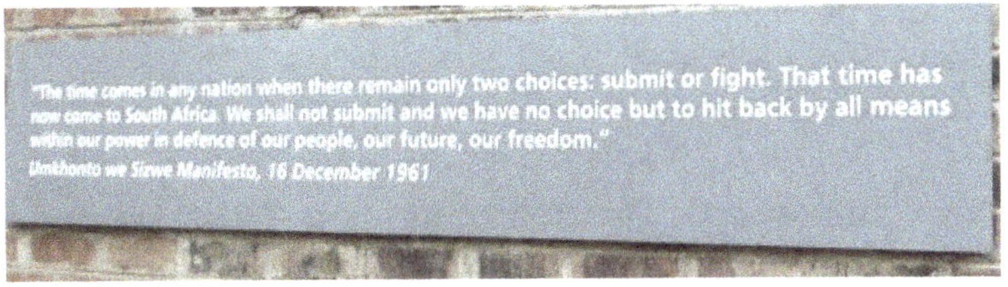

Excerpt from the Umkhonto we Sizwe Manifesto (1961), displayed at Liliesleaf.

The Freedom Charter

The **Freedom Charter** is one of the most essential documents for understanding the soul and the struggle of modern South Africa.

It was not just a political manifesto; it was a **visionary blueprint** for a completely different society, written by the people themselves in direct opposition to the brutality of Apartheid.

Here is a breakdown of the Freedom Charter:

WHAT IS THE FREEDOM CHARTER?

The Freedom Charter is a statement of **core principles** adopted by the **Congress of the People** in Kliptown, outside Johannesburg, on June 25–26, **1955**.

- **The Congress Alliance:** It was a broad, non-racial coalition of anti-apartheid groups, including the **African National Congress (ANC)**, the South African Indian Congress (SAIC), the Coloured People's Congress, and the Congress of Democrats. This unity was central to its power.

- **A People's Document:** The charter was unique because it was compiled from **thousands of demands** solicited from ordinary South Africans—workers, students, peasants, and community members—who sent in their visions for a free South Africa.

The document opens with its most famous and foundational declaration:

"South Africa belongs to all who live in it, black and white, and no government can justly claim authority unless it is based on the will of all the people."

The Charter is divided into ten clauses, which directly challenge the structure of the apartheid state. Key demands include:

- **The People Shall Govern!**

  - Full democracy: the right to vote for all people, regardless of race, colour, or sex.

- **All National Groups Shall Have Equal Rights!**

  - Ending racial segregation and discrimination in all aspects of life (state bodies, courts, and schools).

- **The People Shall Share in the Country's Wealth!**

  - A call for economic justice, including the transfer of mineral wealth, banks, and monopoly industry "to the ownership of the people as a whole." (This clause was highly controversial, even within the alliance).

- **The Land Shall Be Shared Among Those Who Work It!**

  - An end to racial restrictions on land ownership and the re-division of land to banish hunger.

- **All Shall Be Equal Before The Law!**

  - Guaranteed fair trials and the repeal of all discriminatory laws, including the hated Pass Laws.

- **The Doors of Learning and Culture Shall Be Opened!**

  - Free, compulsory, universal, and equal education for all children.

1. **A Unifying Vision:** It provided a **clear, concrete, and inspiring vision** for a non-racial, democratic future, helping to unify the diverse anti-apartheid movement.

2. **Treason Trial:** The apartheid government immediately labelled the charter as a communist plot and used it as evidence in the **Treason Trial (1956–1961)**, where 156 leading activists, including Nelson Mandela, were arrested.

3. **Foundation for the Constitution:** Despite the repression, the Freedom Charter remained the guiding **programmatic document** for the ANC for decades. Its principles, particularly the commitment to equality, human rights, and non-racialism, form the **moral and philosophical foundation** for the democratic **Constitution of South Africa** adopted in 1996.

Understanding the Freedom Charter is essential because it reveals the **aspirations** that motivated the long struggle—a vision of a South Africa built on **social justice and equality**, not just political freedom.

Chapter 4 — Forced Removals During Apartheid

The story of forced removals is one of the most painful chapters in South Africa's past — a time when families were uprooted, communities dismantled, and entire neighborhoods erased by law. These were not distant events; they shaped the lives of millions and altered the geography of the country itself.

Understanding forced removals means confronting the human cost of apartheid, but it also reveals a quieter truth: the remarkable strength of people who rebuilt their lives despite immeasurable loss. This chapter looks at what was taken — and what endured.

4. Forced Removals During Apartheid

Forced removals were one of the most brutal, destructive, and defining aspects of the Apartheid system in South Africa. They represent the systematic policy by which the white minority government physically separated and dispossessed millions of non-white citizens to enforce racial segregation and maintain political and economic control.

Between 1960 and 1983 alone, an estimated **3.5 million people**—Black, Coloured (mixed-race), and Indian South Africans—were forcibly removed from their homes in one of the largest mass evictions in modern history.

The Legal Basis for Removals

Forced removals were implemented under several key pieces of legislation:

- **The Group Areas Act of 1950:** This was the cornerstone of residential apartheid. It provided the legal framework to designate specific urban and suburban areas exclusively for one racial group (White, Black, Coloured, or Indian). Once an area was declared "White," all non-white residents, regardless of how long they had lived there or owned property, were forced to move.

- **The Promotion of Bantu Self-Government Act (1959) & Homeland Policy:** This law established ten "Bantustans" or "Homelands"— tiny, impoverished, and ethnically-defined territories that were designated for Black South Africans. The goal was to strip Black people of their South African citizenship and political rights, declaring them citizens of these pseudo-independent states, regardless of where they actually lived. Forced removals were used to dump millions of people into these overcrowded, underdeveloped Homelands.

Key Types and Examples of Removals

The removals targeted different populations for different reasons:

1. Urban Removals (Implementing the Group Areas Act)

These removals targeted the vibrant, often racially mixed, communities that were too close to or deemed too desirable for white residents.

- **Sophiatown (Johannesburg):** A historically cosmopolitan, politically and culturally vibrant Black suburb. In 1955, thousands of police forcibly removed residents to the newly established townships of Meadowlands and Soweto. Sophiatown was demolished and rebuilt as the white-only suburb of **Triomf** (Afrikaans for "Triumph"). Triomf was next to Westdene and I lived in Westdene for about 2 years. It was also where (RAU) Rand Afrikaans University was situated, now called University of Johannesburg (UJ). After the end of Apartheid its name was returned to Sophiatown.

- **District Six (Cape Town):** A famous, densely populated inner-city area where people of all races (mostly Coloured and Indian) lived together. Declared "White" in 1966, the area was bulldozed, and over 60,000 residents were moved to the barren, distant **Cape Flats**.

2. "Black Spot" Removals

These removals targeted African communities who had legally owned or occupied land in areas designated as "White" South Africa, often for generations (e.g., land surrounded by white-owned farms). The government destroyed these communities and relocated the residents to overcrowded Homelands.

3. Farm Laborer Removals

With the mechanization of agriculture, thousands of Black farm laborers and their families were deemed "superfluous to the labor market" and evicted from white-owned farms, often being dumped into the resettlement camps within the Homelands with no jobs, infrastructure, or services.

The Enduring Legacy

The forced removals created enormous, long-lasting trauma and structural problems that persist in South Africa today:

- **Socio-Economic Inequality:** The removals destroyed established economies, fractured communities, and created the deep, visible pattern of **spatial inequality** that defines South African cities—where poor townships are located far from economic opportunities, and wealthy suburbs remain primarily in the city centers.

- **Land Claims:** After 1994, the **Restitution of Land Rights Act** was passed to allow victims of forced removals to claim their land back or receive compensation, a complex and difficult process that continues today.

Forced removals were, therefore, not just an unfortunate consequence of Apartheid, but a **fundamental pillar** of the system used to consolidate white political and economic power by destroying the social fabric and economic independence of non-white communities.

The period of systematic, large-scale forced removals under the core legislation of **Apartheid officially began to wind down in the _mid-1980s_ and effectively ceased with the repeal of the foundational laws** that enforced them.

The End of Legislative Removals

The policy of forced removals did not have a single, clean end date, but rather faded out as the legal framework of Apartheid collapsed:

1. **Decline in Practice (Mid-1980s):** By the mid-1980s, due to massive **internal resistance** (particularly from the United Democratic Front—UDF) and **intense international pressure**, the government found it increasingly difficult and politically costly to execute large-scale forced removals. Local resistance movements became better organized and more effective at resisting police action.

2. **Repeal of the Group Areas Act (1991):** The key legal pillar that sanctioned the forced separation of races and provided the basis for urban removals was the **Group Areas Act of 1950**. This act was formally **repealed in June 1991** by the apartheid government as part of the initial phase of transition toward democracy. The repeal of this act officially marked the end of the legal power the state had to forcibly relocate entire communities based on race.

3. **Full Democratic Transition (1994):** The political era that enabled the policy finally ended with the **first non-racial democratic election in April 1994**.

The Legacy of Dispossession

While the policy itself stopped in the early 1990s, the struggle over its consequences continued:

- **Land Claims:** The official democratic government, through the **Restitution of Land Rights Act (1994)**, established a legal mechanism for victims of forced removals (those removed after 19 June 1913) to lodge claims for the restoration of their land or for financial compensation. This process is still ongoing today, showing that the effects of the removals are still being addressed.

- **Spatial Inequality:** The urban landscape created by the removals—where poor, non-white townships are located far from city centers and economic hubs—remains the dominant geographic and socio-economic feature of modern South African cities.

In summary, the power and political will to carry out forced removals effectively dissolved in the **late 1980s**, and the legal basis for them was officially eliminated in **1991**.

Chapter 5 — Anglo Boer War

The Anglo Boer War remains one of the defining conflicts in South Africa's history — a struggle that reshaped the land, its people, and its political future. It was a war marked by determination on both sides, but also by harsh tactics, scorched-earth policies, and the tragic legacy of concentration camps. For many South Africans, the effects of this war still echo through memory and identity.

To understand the tensions and alliances that came afterward, it helps to first understand the roots of this conflict and the resilience of those who lived through it.

5. Anglo Boer War

The term **Boer War** usually refers to the **Second Anglo-Boer War (1899–1902)**, a major conflict fought between the British Empire and the two independent Afrikaner republics: The **South African Republic (Transvaal)** and the **Orange Free State**.

The war's history is rooted in over a century of tensions between the British and the Boers (descendants of Dutch settlers, meaning "farmers"), but was ultimately driven by **imperialism** and the control of vast **mineral wealth**.

Causes of the Second Boer War (1899–1902)

The primary triggers for the large-scale conflict were:

- **The Discovery of Gold:** The 1886 discovery of the world's largest gold deposits in the Witwatersrand (Transvaal) fundamentally changed the power dynamic. This immense wealth became the chief prize, fueling British desire to annex the Boer republics.

- **The "Uitlander" Issue:** The gold rush brought a massive influx of foreign workers (**Uitlanders**— mostly British) to the Transvaal. The Boer government, led by President **Paul Kruger**, refused to grant these foreigners voting rights, fearing they would be quickly outnumbered and outvoted, leading to a loss of Boer independence.

- **British Imperialism:** British policy, driven by figures like colonial secretary Joseph Chamberlain and High Commissioner Alfred Milner, was focused on uniting all of Southern Africa under a single British federation. The independent Boer republics were seen as the final obstacle to this ambition.

- **The Jameson Raid (1895):** This failed attempt by a British-backed force to incite an uprising among the Uitlanders solidified Boer mistrust and prompted them to arm heavily.

1. The Boer Offensive (October – December 1899)

The Boers, realizing war was imminent, struck first. Their highly mobile mounted militia (**commandos**) besieged key British-held towns, including **Ladysmith, Mafeking, and Kimberley**. The British suffered heavy, unexpected defeats during a period known as "**Black Week**" in December 1899.

2. The British Counter-Offensive (1900)

The British responded by sending massive reinforcements under the command of **Lord Roberts** and **Lord Kitchener**. They broke the sieges, captured the capital cities of the Boer republics (Bloemfontein and Pretoria), and formally annexed the territories. By the end of 1900, the **conventional phase** of the war was largely over.

3. Guerrilla Warfare and Scorched Earth (1900 – 1902)

The Boers refused to surrender and launched a highly effective **guerrilla campaign** against British supply lines and garrisons. In response, the British adopted harsh counter-insurgency tactics:

- **Blockhouses:** Building thousands of fortified blockhouses to restrict Boer movement.

- **Scorched Earth:** Systematically destroying Boer farms, crops, and livestock to deny the guerrillas supplies and local support.

- **Concentration Camps:** Forcibly relocating over 100,000 **Boer civilians** (mostly women and children) and tens of thousands of **Black Africans** into poorly supplied **concentration camps**. Disease and malnutrition led to the deaths of an estimated **26,000 Boer women and children** and an unknown but significant number of Black Africans.

AFTERMATH AND LEGACY

- **Peace of Vereeniging (May 31, 1902):** The war ended with the signing of this treaty. The Boers accepted British sovereignty in exchange for a promise of future **self-government** and financial aid for reconstruction.

- **Casualties:** The war was costly, resulting in the deaths of approximately 22,000 British soldiers, 7,000 Boer fighters, and tens of thousands of civilians in the camps. Most died from disease.

- **Afrikaner concentration camps**: The exact number of incarcerated victims of the concentration camps for Afrikaners is estimated to number around 40,000 by May 1902, the majority of which were women and children. The total deaths in camps are officially calculated at 27,927 deaths.

- **Union of South Africa:** In 1910, the British granted self-governance to the region, forming the **Union of South Africa**, which incorporated the former Boer republics and the Cape and Natal colonies. This union, however, entrenched racial segregation and eventually laid the political foundation for **Apartheid**.

The two **Boer Wars**, particularly the **Second Anglo-Boer War (1899–1902)**, were pivotal in forming modern South Africa, fundamentally shaping its political structures, economy, and, most tragically, its racial policies.

The war hastened the consolidation of disparate territories and entrenched the racial divisions that defined the 20th century.

1. Political Consolidation (Union of South Africa)

The most direct consequence of the Second Boer War was the unification of the four separate territories into a single state, though under British control.

- **British Victory:** The Treaty of Vereeniging (1902) forced the independent Boer republics (Transvaal and Orange Free State) to accept British sovereignty.

- **Union in 1910:** This paved the way for the British government to unite the four former colonies (Cape Colony, Natal, Transvaal, and Orange River Colony) into the **Union of South Africa in 1910**. This centralized political entity became the modern geographic and administrative framework of the nation.

- **Boer Political Power:** Crucially, the British promised the Boers self-governance, which allowed the **Afrikaners** (descendants of the Boers) to quickly regain political control through democratic processes by forming the **National Party**.

2. Economic Restructuring and Capital

The war solidified the dominance of the mining industry and accelerated industrialization, but on segregated terms.

- **Gold and Capital:** The war was fought largely over the immense gold wealth of the **Witwatersrand**. After the British victory, the mining industry was streamlined and fully integrated into the global financial system, with British and international capital dominating.

- **Infrastructure:** The massive infrastructure developed by the British for military purposes (railways, communications) was repurposed for industrial and mining expansion, further entrenching Johannesburg as the economic hub.

3. The Foundation for Apartheid

The war cemented racial and ethnic divisions, setting the stage for the formal system of Apartheid decades later.

- **The "Native Question":** The Peace of Vereeniging contained a clause (Article 8) stating that the question of granting the franchise (voting rights) to Black Africans would **not** be settled until after the establishment of self-government. This effectively ceded control over racial policy to the white population and **removed Black Africans from the political process** in the newly unified state.

- **White Unity Against Black Majority:** The experience of the war, and the subsequent need to maintain white minority power in the Union of

1910, led to a political accommodation between the former enemies (**Afrikaners and English-speaking whites**). This unity was based on the shared goal of **racial segregation** and ensuring white political and economic dominance.

- **Afrikaner Nationalism:** The trauma of the concentration camps during the war created a powerful, deep-seated sense of victimhood among Afrikaners. This grievance fueled a fervent **Afrikaner nationalism** that eventually led the National Party to victory in 1948 and the formalization of the Apartheid system.

In essence, the Boer War achieved British political aims but created a new, white-dominated state that inherited deep, unresolved racial conflicts, directly leading to the policies that defined South Africa until 1994.

Bloemfontein – Barbed wire tied up to demonstrate the amount of barbed wire being used during the Anglo Boer War, possibly in one concentration camp. Boer War memorial.

Women's Monument (Vrouemonument)
Boer War Memorial – Bloemfontein

Boer War Memorial – Bloemfontein

Boer War Memorial – Bloemfontein

"I WILL NOT LEAVE YOU I WILL NOT FORSAKE YOU"
*The inscription is in **old Dutch/Afrikaans** and translates to a promise of unwavering devotion and support.*

Meaning of the Inscription

The inscription is:

"IK ZAL U NIET BEGEVEN IK ZAL U NIET VERLATEN"

Translation:

This phrase translates directly to:

"I WILL NOT LEAVE YOU I WILL NOT FORSAKE YOU"

Context and Significance

This is a religious and devotional declaration, often quoted or paraphrased from the Bible (specifically, from **Hebrews 13:5** or similar passages in the Old Testament, such as **Joshua 1:5**), where God promises Moses/Joshua that He will not abandon them.

In the context of the **Vrouemonument**, the meaning is threefold:

1. **Divine Assurance:** It serves as a promise of **God's constant presence and support** to the Afrikaner people who suffered immense tragedy during the Second Anglo-Boer War.
2. **National Resilience:** It represents the **unwavering resolve and endurance** of the Boer women who were held in the concentration camps, symbolizing their refusal to abandon their faith or their national identity despite extreme suffering.
3. **Lasting Commemoration:** It signifies the nation's promise to **never forget** the estimated **26,000 women and children** who died in the camps.

The inscription stands above a bronze relief depicting the hardships faced by the women and children in the concentration camps, lending the religious promise a powerful, poignant, and patriotic meaning.

The primary meaning of the inscription at the **Vrouemonument (Women's Memorial) in Bloemfontein** is a solemn **commemoration of the approximately 26,000 Boer women and children** who died in British concentration camps during the Second Anglo-Boer War (1899–1902).

It is arguably the **most emotionally significant memorial to the war** for the Afrikaner people, focusing on civilian tragedy, not military glory.

Graves by the monument
Mathinus Theunis Steyn, 1916
Emily Hobhouse, 1926
Christiaan De Wet, 1922
JD (Vader) Kestell, 1941
Rachel Isabella Steyn [af], 1955

Key Inscription Themes

The central themes of the Vrouemonument's inscriptions and its design reflect **grief, national suffering, and faith.**

1. Commemoration of Civilian Victims

The main inscription is dedicated to the women and children who perished in the camps. It serves as a permanent, visible reminder of the devastating human cost borne by the Afrikaner community due to the British "scorched earth" policy and the subsequent incarceration in the camps.

2. Afrikaner Identity and Resilience

The monument was a powerful force in strengthening **Afrikaner nationalism** in the decades following the war. The sacrifice of the women was framed as a heroic act of martyrdom for the national cause of the independent republics (the Transvaal and the Orange Free State). It symbolized the suffering and resilience of the nation.

3. Religious Dedication

Many Afrikaner memorials include strong religious references. The Vrouemonument, like the **Voortrekker Monument**, ties the national struggle to Christian faith, viewing their survival and ultimate establishment of their identity as divinely sanctioned.

Context

Erected in **1913**, the Vrouemonument was the first official memorial of its kind, predating many other war memorials. It visually centers the suffering of the women and children with a statue group that stands in front of a tall obelisk, emphasizing the profound and often overlooked tragedy of the civilian deaths.

This inscription, written in **Afrikaans/Dutch**, clearly details the monument's dedication and purpose.

Boer War Memorial – Bloemfontein

Original Text (Afrikaans/Dutch)	Translation (English)	Significance
AAN ONZE HELDINNEN EN LIEVE KINDEREN	TO OUR HEROINES AND DEAR CHILDREN	This is the dedication, identifying the people being commemorated—the women and children who suffered during the war.
"UW WIL GESCHIEDE"	"THY WILL BE DONE"	A direct quote from the Lord's Prayer, signifying resignation to God's will and providing comfort and religious context for the immense tragedy.
DIT NATIONAAL MONUMENT IS OPGERICHT TER NAGEDACHTENIS AAN DE	THIS NATIONAL MONUMENT IS ERECTED IN MEMORY OF THE	The statement of purpose for the entire memorial.

Original Text (Afrikaans/Dutch)	Translation (English)	Significance
26370 VROUWEN EN KINDEREN DIE IN DE CONCENTRATIEKAMPEN ZYN OMGEKOMEN	26,370 WOMEN AND CHILDREN WHO DIED IN THE CONCENTRATION CAMPS	This is the crucial historical statistic and the primary reason for the monument's existence, focusing on the civilian tragedy.
EN AAN DE ANDERE VROUWEN EN KINDEREN DIE ELDERS TENGEVOLGE VAN DEN OORLOG 1899-1902 ZYN BEZWEKEN	AND TO THE OTHER WOMEN AND CHILDREN WHO PERISHED ELSEWHERE AS A RESULT OF THE WAR 1899-1902	A broader inclusion of all civilian casualties of the war outside the camps.
ONTHULD 16 DECEMBER 1913	UNVEILED 16 DECEMBER 1913	The date the monument was officially unveiled, which is also the date of the historic Afrikaner holiday, Dingane's Day (now Day of Reconciliation).

One cannot also forget the roughly 20,000 Black African Civilians who also died in the concentration camps.

Overall Significance

The inscription explicitly states that the monument serves as a memorial to the **26,370 Boer women and children who died in the British concentration camps** during the Second Anglo-Boer War.

It frames their deaths as a national sacrifice and martyrdom, establishing the monument as a powerful symbol of **Afrikaner nationalism, suffering, and resilience** against imperial aggression.

The overwhelming majority of people—both soldiers and civilians—who died during the Boer War died from disease, malnutrition, and exposure, rather than from bullets or combat wounds.

This was particularly true for the civilians interned in the British concentration camps.

1. Civilian Deaths in Concentration Camps

The highest death tolls came from the concentration camps established by the British for the internment of Boer women and children, and separately for Black African civilians, as part of their "scorched earth" policy.

Group	Cause of Death	Approximate Fatalities
Boer Civilians	Disease (primarily measles & typhoid), malnutrition, poor sanitation.	26,000 to 28,000
Black African Civilians	Disease, malnutrition, poor sanitation.	14,000 to 20,000+

- **Epidemics:** Overcrowding, inadequate shelter, lack of proper sanitation, and limited medical care created ideal conditions for devastating epidemics, especially **measles** and **typhoid fever.** Children were particularly vulnerable, with tens of thousands of Boer children under 16 dying in the camps.

- **Total Civilian Deaths:** The total estimated civilian death toll is between **40,000 and 48,000** people.

2. British Soldiers

For the British forces, disease was also the largest killer:

British Soldier Fatalities	Number	% of Total Deaths
Died of Disease	~14,000	~65%
Killed in Action/Died of Wounds	~8,000	~35%

- **The Main Culprit: Typhoid fever** and **dysentery** ran rampant through the poorly sanitized British military camps, often paralyzing entire columns of troops. In fact, more British soldiers died from disease than were killed by the enemy.

The horrific mortality rates from disease, particularly in the concentration camps, created a massive political scandal in Britain and ultimately highlighted the devastating, non-combat costs of the war. ~ 65%

This fact—that disease, not combat, was the primary killer—is a stark reminder of the often-unseen human catastrophe of that conflict.

Bok van Blerk - De la Rey

The song **"De La Rey"** by South African singer **Bok van Blerk** is about **Koos de la Rey** (Jacobus Herculaas de la Rey), one of the most brilliant and respected generals of the **Boer forces** during the Second Anglo-Boer War (1899–1902).

The song is a powerful Afrikaner anthem that uses historical figures and references to comment on the contemporary state of South Africa.

Meaning of the Song

The song operates on two main levels:

1. Historical Tribute

The lyrics directly address General Koos de la Rey, calling him to return and lead the Afrikaner people once more. It romanticizes De la Rey's leadership during the war.

- **The Fighter:** De la Rey was a key figure in the **Boer commando's guerrilla campaign** against the overwhelming forces of the British Empire. He was known for his strategic military genius, his deep religious faith, and his humanitarian treatment of prisoners.

- **The Symbol of Resistance:** By invoking De la Rey, the song celebrates the heroic, defiant spirit of the Boer forces who refused to surrender and instead fought for their independence (*vryheid*—freedom).

2. Contemporary Frustration and Identity

The song struck a deep chord with many Afrikaners (the descendants of the Boers) because it channeled a sense of **cultural displacement, political frustration, and anxiety** in modern, democratic South Africa.

- **Sense of Loss:** The song expresses a feeling that the Afrikaner identity and cultural heritage are under threat or being marginalized in the post-Apartheid era.

- **A Call for Leadership:** The repeated call for De la Rey to "return" is not a literal call for a military uprising, but a metaphorical plea for a leader to emerge and inspire the Afrikaner community to reclaim a sense of pride, direction, and safety in the new South Africa.

- **Controversy:** The song's massive popularity and emotional intensity caused some controversy when released (2007), as critics from outside the Afrikaner community feared it promoted reactionary nationalism or a desire to return to the political dominance of the past. The singer and fans, however, generally defended it as a legitimate expression of cultural identity and historical pride.

In short, "De La Rey" is an emotional folk song that connects a pivotal figure from the past to the modern-day concerns about Afrikaner political and cultural identity in the "Rainbow Nation."

Chapter 6 — Nelson Mandela

Nelson Mandela's story is inseparable from the story of South Africa itself. His journey — from young activist to political prisoner to the nation's first democratic president — captures both the suffering of apartheid and the extraordinary hope that followed. Mandela was not perfect, but he was principled, disciplined, and unwavering in his belief that the country could choose a better path.

To understand South Africa's transition into democracy, one must understand the man whose courage helped make it possible.

Nelson Mandela, 2008.

Photo by South Africa The Good News /
www.sagoodnews.co.za.
Licensed under **CC BY 2.0**
(https://creativecommons.org/licenses/by/2.0/).

6. Nelson Mandela

Nelson Mandela's significance to South Africa is immense; he is considered the **founding father of democratic South Africa** and a global icon of peace and reconciliation. His life and work were the driving force behind ending **Apartheid** and establishing a non-racial democracy.

Key Areas of Significance

1. The End of Apartheid and Transition to Democracy

Mandela provided the indispensable leadership that guided South Africa from a racially segregated state to a free democracy.

- **Symbol of Resistance:** Before his release, Mandela, through his 27 years of imprisonment (18 of which were spent on Robben Island), became the most powerful **international symbol of the anti-Apartheid struggle**. His image gave global legitimacy and moral weight to the movement.

- **Negotiator of Change:** Upon his release in 1990, he led the African National Congress (ANC) in complex and fraught negotiations with the Apartheid government, led by President F.W. de Klerk. These negotiations were instrumental in dismantling discriminatory laws and establishing the framework for a democratic transition.

- **First Democratic President (1994):** He became South Africa's first democratically elected president in the country's first truly non-racial election. This event symbolized the definitive end of white minority rule and the beginning of the "Rainbow Nation."

2. Reconciliation and Nation-Building

Mandela's greatest legacy lies in his commitment to **reconciliation** over retribution, preventing a civil war in the transition period.

- **Forgiveness:** He famously preached forgiveness toward the white minority who had imprisoned him. He used symbols, like embracing the captain of the Springboks (the white-dominated national rugby team), to visually demonstrate national unity.

- **Truth and Reconciliation Commission (TRC):** He established the TRC, chaired by Archbishop Desmond Tutu, which aimed not for criminal prosecution but for truth-telling. This process allowed victims and perpetrators of Apartheid-era crimes to share their stories in exchange for conditional amnesty, a unique mechanism designed to heal the deep wounds of the past.

3. Global Moral Authority

Mandela transcended national politics to become a universal figure.

- **Human Rights Champion:** He demonstrated that peaceful transition and moral leadership could overcome systemic oppression, influencing liberation movements and peace processes worldwide.

- **Global Conscience:** Even after retirement, he used his platform to advocate for social justice issues, notably HIV/AIDS awareness and children's rights, solidifying his role as a global elder statesman and a moral conscience for the world.

Mandela's significance is thus not just historical, but continuous; his commitment to non-racialism and constitutional democracy remains the foundational standard and a constant challenge for modern South Africa.

Moss Mashishi, Peter Mokaba - President of SAYCO and the original 'Young Lion', Mandela, June Sinclair (Dep Vice Chancellor), Khaya Ngema, and David Storey at **Wits University** *after the release of Nelson Mandela around 1990 under the banner of NUSAS – National Union of South African Students.*

©David Storey, used with permission.

Chapter 7 — All Roads Lead to Johannesburg

In South Africa, all movement — economic, political, or personal — seems to circle back to Johannesburg. It is the crossroads where opportunity meets challenge, where people from every province converge to build careers, seek education, or simply try their luck. Whether you come by road, rail, or air, Johannesburg stands as the country's central gateway — a place that can overwhelm at first, yet reveals its rhythm once you understand it. This chapter explores Johannesburg's central role in South Africa, shaped by gold, migration, ambition, and the economic forces that continue to draw people toward it.

7. All Roads lead to Johannesburg

Illustrative representation of Johannesburg's skyline.

The phrase "All roads lead to Johannesburg" is a variation of the famous ancient proverb, **"All roads lead to Rome."** The variation is a modern, metaphorical acknowledgment of **Johannesburg's overwhelming economic and cultural dominance** in South Africa and, to a large extent, in Southern Africa.

Meaning and Significance

The original proverb about Rome signifies that a single, powerful center influences all paths and endeavors. When applied to Johannesburg, the meaning is that the city is the **ultimate destination** for anyone seeking:

- **Economic Opportunity:** Johannesburg is the **financial, commercial, and industrial heart** of South Africa and often acts as the gateway to the African continent's economy. People from across the region and the continent migrate to Johannesburg in search of better jobs, higher wages, and economic advancement.

- **Career and Education:** It hosts major corporate headquarters, specialized industries, and world-class universities, making it the primary place to pursue advanced careers and education.

- **Infrastructure Hub:** As the largest city in the landlocked Gauteng province, Johannesburg is the hub for **transportation and logistics** in Southern Africa, with major highways, railway lines, and the busiest airport on the continent (O.R. Tambo International Airport) converging there.

Essentially, the saying reflects the historical reality that, for over a century since the discovery of gold, Johannesburg has been the powerful **magnet** drawing people and capital toward it.

Johannesburg is big and sprawling, a city that is a work in progress. Despite its history - or maybe because of it - it's a city with a youthful vibe that is constantly changing and has a hip fashion and arts scene to match.

Johannesburg is the economic engine of South Africa, and an important financial and business center for all of the African continent. Jo'burg, as it is affectionately called, is also a very green city; about six million trees were planted within the city to create one of the world's largest urban forests.

Chapter 8 — Cape Town

Cape Town is often described as one of the most beautiful cities in the world — a place where mountains, coastline, and layered history meet in a single, striking landscape. Yet beyond the postcard views lies a city shaped by its own contrasts: communities divided and reconnected over time, reminders of the past standing beside signs of renewal. Cape Town draws visitors for its scenery, but it reveals much more to those who look closely. This chapter offers an honest look at a city that is as complex as it is breathtaking.

8. Cape Town

Illustrative representation of Cape Town.

The history of **Cape Town** is distinct from the rest of South Africa, as it was the site of the **first permanent European settlement** in the region, fundamentally shaping its political, cultural, and geographic development.

Early Exploration and Indigenous People

- **Khoisan:** Long before European arrival, the area was inhabited by the **Khoikhoi** (pastoralists) and the **San** (hunter-gatherers), collectively known as the Khoisan.

- **European Discovery:** The Portuguese explorer **Bartolomeu Dias** rounded the Cape in 1488, naming it the "Cape of Storms." Later, it was renamed the **Cape of Good Hope** as it offered the possibility of a sea route to the East. However, no permanent European settlement was established for over a century due to dangerous conditions.

The Dutch Colonial Era (1652 – 1795)

- **Permanent Settlement:** The modern history of Cape Town begins in **1652** when **Jan van Riebeeck**, an administrator for the **Dutch East India Company (VOC)**, established a **refreshment station** at the Cape of Good Hope. Its purpose was to supply VOC ships traveling between the Netherlands and the East Indies (Indonesia).

- **Expansion and Slavery:** The settlement quickly expanded beyond a simple fort and vegetable garden. The need for labor led to the importation of **slaves** from Indonesia, Madagascar, India, and parts of Africa. This influx of diverse enslaved peoples gave rise to the **Cape Malay** community and profoundly shaped the cultural, linguistic (Afrikaans), and genetic makeup of the region.

- **Conflict:** European expansion inland led to continuous **conflict with the indigenous Khoisan** populations, whose land and traditional way of life were aggressively disrupted.

The British Takeover (1795 – 1910)

- **Strategic Acquisition:** Britain seized the Cape Colony from the Dutch twice (briefly in 1795 and permanently in 1806) during the Napoleonic Wars. The Cape was a vital strategic naval base safeguarding the route to India.

- **British Influence:** The British established English as the primary language of government and commerce and introduced major administrative changes. They were instrumental in the formal **abolition of slavery in 1834**, which dramatically altered the colony's labor market.

- **Racial Policy:** Unlike the Boer republics in the north, the Cape Colony operated under a system of **qualified franchise** where some non-white men could vote based on property ownership, though this was systematically eroded over time.

20th Century: Urban Growth and Apartheid

- **Union and Growth:** Cape Town became the **legislative capital** when the Union of South Africa was formed in 1910, housing the Parliament. It continued to grow as a major port and center for trade and tourism.

- **Apartheid Impact:** The city suffered deeply under Apartheid (1948–1994). The implementation of the **Group Areas Act** led to the forced removal of thousands of non-white residents from central, desirable neighborhoods like **District Six** to segregated townships on the sandy Cape Flats, scarring the urban landscape.

- **Mandela's Release:** Cape Town was the site of a globally symbolic event: **Nelson Mandela's release from prison in 1990**. He delivered his first public address as a free man from the balcony of the City Hall.

Today, Cape Town is celebrated for its natural beauty and serves as a major tourist and technological hub, but it continues to grapple with the spatial and economic inequalities imposed by its colonial and Apartheid past.

Chapter 9 — The University of the Witwatersrand (Wits)

The University of the Witwatersrand — known simply as Wits — is more than an academic institution; it is one of the intellectual anchors of South Africa. Located in the heart of Johannesburg, Wits has shaped generations of thinkers, professionals, and leaders who went on to influence the country's political, cultural, and scientific landscape. Its history reflects both the challenges and the progress of the nation itself.

This chapter looks at what makes Wits a defining part of Johannesburg's identity and a respected name across the country.

9. The University of the Witwatersrand (Wits)

The **University of the Witwatersrand (Wits)** is highly important to South Africa for three primary reasons: its **pivotal role in the nation's economy** (rooted in mining), its tradition of **academic excellence and research**, and its consistent, often perilous, stand against **Apartheid**.

Wits Campus

1. Economic Foundation and Location

Wits' importance is intrinsically linked to the history of Johannesburg itself.

- **Mining Roots:** The university originated as the **South African School of Mines** in 1896, established to serve the burgeoning diamond and gold industries. This connection positioned Wits at the forefront of engineering, geology, and technology vital for South Africa's primary economic engine.

- **Economic Hub:** Located in the heart of **Johannesburg** (the economic powerhouse of the continent), Wits has consistently supplied the leadership, accountants, engineers, and scientists necessary to sustain and grow the nation's financial and industrial sectors.

2. Role in Academic and Research Excellence

Wits is a leading research university in Africa, contributing significantly to global knowledge.

- **Pioneering Research:** The university has a long list of academic "firsts" in South Africa, including being the first to have a nuclear accelerator and a computer, and pioneering work in developing radar during WWII.

- **Scientific Breakthroughs:** Wits scholars have made globally significant contributions in areas like **human origins and evolution** (with the discovery of famous hominid fossils in the nearby Sterkfontein Caves) and advancements in health sciences and deep-level mining.

- **Nobel Laureates:** Wits has a high number of Nobel Prize-affiliated individuals who have studied or taught there, including **Nelson Mandela** (Peace), **Nadine Gordimer** (Literature), **Aaron Klug** (Chemistry), and **Sydney Brenner** (Physiology or Medicine).

3. Anti-Apartheid Activism

Wits earned a reputation as a major institutional opponent of the Apartheid regime, defending the principles of an "open university."

- **Open Admission:** Even after the government passed the **Extension of University Education Act of 1959** (which legally enforced segregation), Wits continually affirmed its commitment to the principle of "academic non-segregation," defying government policy.

- **Hub of Protest:** The campus was a central location for resistance, debate, and intellectual challenge to the regime. Its students and staff faced **banning, detention, and police raids** for their activism.

- **Transition and Constitution:** Wits served as a hub for critical thinking during the transition to democracy. Academics and alumni were deeply involved in drafting the **Constitution of South Africa**, and Wits graduates served as the first two Chief Justices of the democratic nation.

Academic Excellence

The University of the Witwatersrand has cemented its reputation as one of Africa's premier institutions of higher learning. Established in 1922, Wits has consistently been at the forefront of academic achievement and research innovation. The university's

rich history is marked by notable alumni,
groundbreaking research, and significant contributions
to various fields of study.

Strategic Location

Situated in the heart of Johannesburg, Wits enjoys a
strategic location that is easily accessible from major
transport hubs. The university is well-connected to
public transportation, making it convenient for both
local and international participants to reach the venue.
Its central location also means that participants have
access to the city's numerous attractions, amenities, and
cultural sites.

Cultural and Intellectual Hub

As a leading institution in Africa, Wits is a cultural and
intellectual hub that attracts scholars, researchers, and
students from around the world. The university's
diverse and vibrant community creates an environment
conducive to intellectual exchange and collaboration.

Commitment to Social Justice

Wits has a storied history of commitment to social
justice and activism. The university played a significant
role in the anti-apartheid movement, and its legacy of
advocating for equality and human rights continues to
this day. This ethos aligns perfectly with the objectives

of the **Pan-African Universities Debating Championship (PAUDC)**, which aims to promote intellectual engagement and foster cross-cultural exchange.

Innovative Research and Academic Programmes

Wits is renowned for its innovative research and academic programs that address some of the most pressing challenges facing the continent and the world. The university's strong emphasis on interdisciplinary research and collaboration ensures that it remains at the cutting edge of knowledge creation. Participants in PAUDC 2025 will benefit from this environment of academic rigor and intellectual curiosity.

Vibrant Campus Life

The vibrant campus life at Wits offers participants a dynamic and engaging atmosphere. The university hosts numerous cultural, social, and academic events throughout the year, providing a rich tapestry of experiences for students and visitors alike.

During PAUDC 2025, participants will have the opportunity to immerse themselves in this vibrant campus culture, making their experience truly memorable. In summary, the University of the Witwatersrand is not just an academic institution; it's a beacon of excellence, diversity, and intellectual engagement. Hosting PAUDC 2025 at Wits ensures a high-quality, impactful, and enriching experience for all participants.

The period between **1985 and 1994** was arguably the most volatile and politically critical time in Wits University's history. It was a decade of intense **anti-Apartheid activism, confrontation with the state, and a visible demographic shift** as the country hurtled toward democracy. I studied through those years – studying until 1991, and then leaving to work until I had time to finish my degree, and finally graduating in 1995, after the first democratic all race elections in South Africa.

Wits transformed from a liberal-leaning, predominantly white institution into a key battleground and intellectual hub for the end of Apartheid.

The Nexus of Anti-Apartheid Protest

Wits was one of the few historically white universities to formally maintain a position as an **"open university"** (admitting Black students, though in small numbers initially) and became a central site of organized political resistance.

- **Frontline Activism:** The campus and its surrounding area (Braamfontein) were constantly involved in political action. Students and faculty participated in **mass meetings,**

protests, and demonstrations against apartheid policies, rent increases, and political detentions.

- **Confrontation with the State:** The campus was repeatedly invaded by **riot police** and security forces who used batons, tear gas, and sometimes live ammunition to break up peaceful gatherings. This made campus life highly tense and often dangerous.

- **Political Alliances:** Students' organizations, such as the **National Union of South African Students (NUSAS)** and the **Azanian Student Organisation (AZASO)**, formed strong alliances with the broader resistance movement, particularly the **United Democratic Front (UDF)**, linking campus issues directly to national political struggles.

Academic Environment and Intellectual Resistance

The university served as a sanctuary for critical thought and academic opposition to the regime.

- **Critical Inquiry:** Academics actively challenged apartheid ideology and policy, particularly in the humanities and social sciences. Many scholars were involved in research projects that directly **critiqued the apartheid system** and provided support for marginalized communities.

- **Cost of Dissent:** Many staff and students faced severe consequences for their activism, including **detention without trial, banning orders, surveillance, and deportation**.

- **Growth and Diversity:** By 1985, student numbers had grown significantly (to over 16,000), and while still predominantly white, the presence of Black students increased steadily. This growing diversity, though constrained by apartheid laws, further fueled the internal push for non-racial policies and the dismantling of the segregation system.

The Transition Period (1990–1994)

The period following the unbanning of the ANC and the release of Nelson Mandela in 1990 marked a shift from outright confrontation to political engagement.

- **Hub for Debate:** Wits served as a critical hub for **debate and engagement** during the formal transition period. Academics, lawyers, and political scientists from the university were deeply involved in the complex **constitutional negotiations** that paved the way for the 1994 democratic elections.

- **Legacy of Leadership:** This period cemented Wits' reputation as an institution that produced intellectual leaders for the new democracy. Notably, Wits graduates were instrumental in the drafting of the Constitution, and Wits alumni went on to serve as the first two Chief Justices of democratic South Africa.

In summary, Wits between 1985 and 1994 was defined by a constant tension between **academic commitment to an open society and the brutal realities of the dying apartheid state**, making it a truly revolutionary space.

Wits University

Wits University campus mural — Johannesburg

Chapter 10 — Durban/KwaZulu-Natal

Durban and the wider KwaZulu-Natal (KZN) offer a different rhythm from the country's interior — a blend of warm Indian Ocean beaches, rich Zulu heritage, and a climate that makes outdoor life part of everyday living. Yet, like much of South Africa, the region carries layers of history that shaped its people and its identity, from early settlements to modern political and cultural life. Durban is both a relaxed coastal city and a place of significant historical depth.

This chapter explores what gives KZN its unique character within the South African landscape.

10. Durban/ Kwazulu Natal

Durban, the largest city in the province of KwaZulu-Natal (KZN), holds immense importance to South Africa, primarily due to its economic gateway status, its unique cultural heritage, and its role as a major domestic and international tourism hub.

Here is a breakdown of why Durban is so significant:

1. Economic Gateway: The Port of Durban

Durban's single most critical role is defined by its massive port, often referred to as the **busiest and largest shipping terminal in sub-Saharan Africa.**

- **Trade Hub:** The Port of Durban handles over **60% of South Africa's containerized cargo** and is the main maritime gateway for the entire Southern African region. It is a vital link for South Africa's international trade with the Far East, Middle East, and Europe.

- **Link to the Industrial Heartland:** The port serves as the crucial point of entry and exit for the **Witwatersrand industrial region** (Gauteng, including Johannesburg). Bulk raw materials, capital goods, and industrial equipment are imported here, while goods like coal and minerals are exported, often traveling via pipeline and rail to and from Johannesburg.

- **Manufacturing:** Durban is the **second most important manufacturing hub** in South Africa, specializing in automotive production, chemicals, and agribusiness. The efficiency of the port directly impacts the viability of these large industrial sectors.

2. Unique Cultural and Demographic Hub

Durban's history of migration has created a distinctive and globally significant cultural landscape.

- **Indian Heritage:** Durban has one of the largest concentrations of people of **Indian descent outside of India.** This population originated largely from **indentured labourers** brought by the British in the 1860s to work on sugarcane plantations.

- This heritage gives Durban its unique character, reflected in its cuisine (especially the famous **Durban curry** and **bunny chow**), large mosques (like the Juma Masjid), and vibrant Hindu temples and festivals (like Diwali).

- **Zulu Heartland:** Durban sits on the coast of **KwaZulu-Natal**, the heartland of the **Zulu nation**—South Africa's largest ethnic group. The city is a major center for Zulu culture, politics, and urban life, blending traditional influences with a modern city context.

Durban City by the sea on the Indian Ocean.

3. Tourism and Lifestyle

The city's geography and climate make it South Africa's premier holiday destination for many locals and a draw for international visitors.

- **The Golden Mile:** Durban is famed for its long stretch of golden beaches, known as the **Golden Mile**, which, unlike the cold water of Cape Town, is washed by the warm waters of the **Indian Ocean**, making swimming popular year-round.

- **Gateway to Reserves:** It is the main entry point for tourists seeking to explore KwaZulu-Natal's renowned game and nature reserves, including the historic **Zulu Battlefields** and the **Drakensberg Mountains**.

- **Infrastructure:** The city has invested heavily in tourism infrastructure, including the International Convention Centre (ICC) and the Moses Mabhida Stadium (built for the 2010 FIFA World Cup), solidifying its role as a destination for major international conferences and sporting events.

Traditional handcrafts and souvenirs for sale at a Durban market.

Durban remains one of South Africa's most visited coastal cities, combining natural beauty with vibrant urban development.

Moses Mabhida Stadium — Durban's iconic multi-purpose venue.

Interior décor of a South African guesthouse in Durban North — showcasing the country's eclectic style and warm color palette.

Breakers Resort, Umhlanga — offering a contrasting view of coastal accommodation along KwaZulu-Natal's popular Dolphin Coast.

The history of the **Zulu people** is one of the most powerful and dramatic in Southern Africa, marked by rapid military expansion, the creation of a powerful kingdom, and fierce resistance against colonial powers.

Illustrative representation of a traditional African cultural gathering.

I. Origins and Early Clan Life

- **Nguni Ancestry:** The Zulu originated from the **Nguni** communities, who migrated southward down the east coast of Africa over centuries as part of the wider Bantu migrations.

- **Minor Clan:** The Zulu were initially a relatively minor clan in what is now northern KwaZulu-Natal, founded around the early 17th century by **Zulu kaMalandela**. The name Zulu means "heaven" or "sky" in the isiZulu language.

- **Small Chiefdoms:** Before the 19th century, the region was characterized by a patchwork of small, independent Nguni chiefdoms living mostly agricultural lives, occasionally engaging in skirmishes over land and cattle.

II. The Rise of the Zulu Kingdom (Shaka Zulu)

The transformation of the small Zulu clan into a powerful kingdom is inextricably linked to the figure of **Shaka kaSenzangakhona (Shaka Zulu)**.

- **Shaka's Ascent (c. 1816):** Shaka was the son of a Zulu chief but was initially exiled. He served as a brilliant warrior under the powerful Mthethwa Paramountcy. Upon his father's death, he successfully claimed the Zulu chieftaincy with military backing.

- **Military Revolution:** Shaka revolutionized warfare in the region. He:

  - Replaced the long throwing spear with the **iklwa** (a short, stabbing spear) designed for close combat.

  - Instituted the **Regimental System (Amabutho)** based on age-groups, creating a highly disciplined standing army.

  - Developed the famous **"Bull's Horns"** formation (a military tactic of encirclement).

- **The Mfecane (The Crushing):** Shaka's aggressive expansion led to a period of widespread upheaval and devastating conflict across Southern Africa known as the **Mfecane** (or Difaqane, meaning "the crushing"). Chiefdoms were shattered, populations fled, and new states (like the Ndebele) were formed by groups fleeing or breaking away from the Zulu. By his death in 1828, Shaka had forged the **Zulu Kingdom** into the dominant power in the region.

King Tshaka Statue

III. Conflict with European Settlers

The Zulu Kingdom's strength meant that, unlike many other African groups, they were not immediately overwhelmed by European settlement.

- **Voortrekker Clash:** Following Shaka's assassination by his half-brothers, his successor **Dingane** clashed violently with the **Voortrekkers** (Boer settlers migrating inland from the Cape Colony). The defeat of Dingane at the **Battle of Blood River (1838)** led to the Boers establishing the short-lived Republic of Natalia.

- **British Annexation:** The British annexed the Natal region in 1843, pushing the Zulu Kingdom back north of the Tugela River.

IV. The Anglo-Zulu War (1879)

The independent Zulu Kingdom, under **King Cetshwayo**, became the last major obstacle to Britain's ambition to unify all of Southern Africa.

- **British Ultimatum:** In 1878, the British High Commissioner Sir Bartle Frere issued an impossible ultimatum to Cetshwayo, demanding the disbandment of the Zulu army.

- **Isandlwana:** When Cetshwayo refused, the British invaded in January 1879. The war began with a shocking Zulu victory at the **Battle of Isandlwana**, where the Zulu impi (army) annihilated a large, modern British force.

- **Defeat:** Despite this early win, the superior technology and overwhelming numbers of the reinforced British army eventually led to the decisive defeat of the Zulu at the **Battle of Ulundi** in July 1879. King Cetshwayo was captured, and the kingdom was fragmented into 13 smaller chiefdoms, leading to internal strife and the eventual British annexation of Zululand in 1887.

V. The Zulu in Modern South Africa

- **Apartheid Era:** Under the Apartheid system, the Zulu homeland was consolidated into the **KwaZulu Bantustan**. Despite this artificial administrative structure, the Zulu retained a strong sense of cultural identity and royal tradition.

- **Post-Apartheid:** Today, the **Zulu King** remains a ceremonial, cultural, and spiritual leader of the Zulu nation. Zulu culture, language (isiZulu), and history remain a vibrant and integral part of the South African national identity.

Chapter 11 — Xhosa People

The Xhosa people form one of South Africa's major cultural groups, known for their deep traditions, expressive languages, and strong sense of identity. Their history is intertwined with that of the Eastern Cape, where generations have shaped the region's political, spiritual, and social life. From clan structures to initiation customs and the distinctive beauty of isiXhosa, their culture remains a vital thread in the country's fabric.

This chapter offers an introduction to the Xhosa people and the role they continue to play in South Africa today.

11. Xhosa people

The history of the Xhosa people is one of the most significant and well-documented of all South African groups. It is a narrative of migration, complex social structure, fierce wars of resistance against European colonial expansion, and central involvement in the anti-Apartheid struggle. Nelson Mandela was born in the Transkei and was ethnically Xhosa.

I. Origins and Early Society

- **Nguni Migration**: The Xhosa, like the Zulu, belong to the wider Nguni branch of the Bantu-speaking peoples. They migrated southwards, arriving in what is now the Eastern Cape region of South Africa centuries ago.

- **Geographic Settlement**: The Xhosa settled along the coast and inland areas east of the Great Fish River, living as pastoralists and mixed farmers.

- **Social Structure**: Xhosa society was highly structured, based on a hierarchy of chiefdoms (*amakhosi*) who ruled over clans (*iziduko*). Clan membership is crucial, and the Xhosa traditionally trace their lineage through the paternal line.

- **Cultural Identity**: Xhosa culture is known for its intricate rites of passage, especially the male initiation ceremony (*ulwaluko*), and the distinctive click sounds in their language, isiXhosa.

II. The Frontier Wars (The Mfecane and Wars of Resistance)

From the late 18th century to the late 19th century, the Xhosa people were involved in a series of conflicts with European settlers (both Dutch and British), known collectively as the Xhosa Wars or Cape Frontier Wars (nine wars fought between 1779 and 1878).

- **Conflict Over Land**: The wars were primarily fought over control of the fertile grazing lands between the Great Fish River and the Kei River. The advancing European settlers repeatedly encroached upon Xhosa territory.

- **British Annexation**: The British, having taken control of the Cape Colony in 1806, relentlessly pushed the colonial boundary eastward, leading to major conflicts that devastated Xhosa society and livestock.

- **The Mfecane (Early 19th Century)**: Xhosa society was also destabilized by the wider regional conflicts and migrations stemming from the rise of the Zulu Kingdom, which impacted their northern borders.

III. The Cattle Killing Prophecy (1856–1857)

This event is one of the most tragic and misunderstood periods in Xhosa history.

- **The Prophetess**: A young prophetess named Nongqawuse claimed to have received a message from ancestors stating that if the Xhosa people killed all their cattle and destroyed their crops, the ancestors would rise up and drive the British into the sea.

- **Devastation**: Driven by spiritual conviction and desperation after years of war and cattle disease, large numbers of Xhosa chiefs and followers obeyed. The result was a catastrophic famine that led to the death of tens of thousands of people and the total collapse of the independent Xhosa resistance movements, allowing the British to solidify their colonial control over the region.

IV. Apartheid and Modern South Africa

- **Forced Migrations**: The Xhosa territories were ultimately consolidated under the Apartheid government into two politically-constructed Bantustans (or "homelands"): the Transkei and the Ciskei. These were impoverished, politically dependent, and used to deny Xhosa people South African citizenship.

- **Role in Resistance**: Despite their fragmentation, the Xhosa people played an overwhelmingly central role in the resistance against Apartheid.

  - Many of the founding leaders of the African National Congress (ANC), including Nelson Mandela and Oliver Tambo, were Xhosa.

  - Steve Biko, the founder of the Black Consciousness Movement, was also Xhosa, originating from the Eastern Cape.

Today, the Eastern Cape remains the cultural heartland of the Xhosa people, whose history of resilience and struggle is foundational to South Africa's modern identity.

Illustrative representation of traditional African ceremonial attire.

With Friends Thomas Hlongwane and Kingsley Ansong back from Cape Town, about half way near Colesburg – 255 Km from Bloemfontein. Thomas was from Soweto, and Kingsley from Ghana. Kingsley used to cut hair in the center of Johannesburg in around 1999.

Chapter 12 — Twelve Official Languages

Few countries in the world can claim the linguistic richness that South Africa holds. With twelve official languages spoken across its provinces, the country's identity is shaped by a tapestry of voices — each carrying its own history, rhythm, and worldview. These languages are more than a means of communication; they reflect the diverse cultures and communities that make up the nation.

This chapter offers a clear introduction to South Africa's linguistic landscape and the role these languages play in everyday life.

12. Twelve Official Languages

South Africa is one of the most linguistically diverse countries in the world, recognizing **twelve official languages** to ensure equal status and promote multilingualism.

The Twelve Official Languages

The official languages of South Africa fall into two main groups: the **Nguni** and **Sotho** groups (Bantu languages), and the **Germanic** group (Indo-European languages).

Language Family	Official Language	Key Facts and Spoken Areas
Nguni	Zulu (isiZulu)	The most widely spoken home language. Predominant in KwaZulu-Natal (KZN).
Nguni	Xhosa (isiXhosa)	The second most spoken home language. Predominant in the Eastern and Western Cape.
Nguni	Ndebele (isiNdebele)	Spoken primarily in the Mpumalanga province.
Nguni	Swazi (siSwati)	Spoken near the Eswatini (Swaziland) border, particularly in Mpumalanga.

Language Family	Official Language	Key Facts and Spoken Areas
Sotho	Sepedi (Northern Sotho)	Predominant in the Limpopo province.
Sotho	Sesotho (Southern Sotho)	Predominant in the Free State province.
Sotho	Setswana (Tswana)	Spoken in the North West province, bordering Botswana.
Venda	Tshivenda	Spoken predominantly in the Limpopo province.
Tsonga	Xitsonga	Spoken in the Limpopo and Mpumalanga provinces.
Germanic	Afrikaans	Evolved from 17th-century Dutch. Widely spoken in the Northern, Western, and Eastern Cape provinces.
Germanic	English	The main language of government, commerce, and media, though only the 7th most common home language.
Sign Language	South African Sign Language (SASL)	Added as the 12th official language in 2023, granting it the same status as spoken languages.

Linguistic Reality

While English is the primary language of official documents, business, and higher education, the majority of South Africans speak an indigenous African language at home.

- **Most Common Home Languages (*by percentage*):**

    1. **isiZulu**

    2. **isiXhosa**

    3. **Afrikaans**

    4. **Sepedi**

- **Code-Switching:** It is very common for South Africans to be multilingual and to switch between two or more languages in a single conversation (a practice called **code-switching**). For instance, combining Zulu and English words is a widespread urban phenomenon.

English is highly important in South Africa, even though it's only the seventh most common home language. Its significance stems from its historical role, its function as a **lingua franca**, and its dominance in key sectors of modern society.

Role as the Lingua Franca

In a country with twelve official languages, English acts as the neutral and functional language of communication across diverse groups.

- **Inter-Ethnic Communication:** English is often the only common language understood by people from different cultural and linguistic backgrounds (e.g., between a Zulu speaker and an Afrikaans speaker). It serves as the primary bridge for national discourse.

- **Media and Social Discourse:** It is the dominant language used in major national newspapers, magazines, television news broadcasts, and online media, making it central to public life and political debate.

Importance in Key Sectors

English holds a near-monopoly in the most powerful institutions of the country, granting it enormous economic and academic influence.

- **Commerce and Finance:** Johannesburg is the financial heart of Africa, and almost all major business, banking, trade, and international dealings are conducted in **English**. Proficiency in English is essential for upward mobility in the corporate sector.

- **Higher Education:** While many universities strive for multilingualism, the vast majority of

lectures, textbooks, research, and technical papers at the tertiary level (universities) are delivered and written in English.

- **Government and Law:** While the constitution mandates equality for all twelve languages, English is the primary language used for parliamentary debate, government administration, legal contracts, and the courts.

Global Connectivity

English provides South Africa with a direct link to the international community.

- **International Relations:** English is the standard language for diplomacy, international trade, tourism, and communication with organizations like the United Nations, Commonwealth, and the African Union.

- **Digital Access:** It is the default language of the internet, making it crucial for accessing global information, technological resources, and participating in the global digital economy.

In essence, while indigenous languages maintain cultural and personal importance, **English is the working language of power, economy, and national integration** in South Africa.

Chapter 13 — Sport in South Africa

Sport is woven deeply into South African life — a source of national pride, community identity, and moments of unity that often rise above the country's divisions. From rugby and cricket to football and athletics, sporting achievements have shaped how South Africans see themselves and how the world sees them. These events are not just competitions; they are shared experiences that reflect the country's history, challenges, and hopes.

This chapter looks at the central role sport plays in South Africa's cultural landscape.

13. Sport in South Africa

Sport is deeply embedded in the culture of South Africa, acting as a powerful force for national identity and reconciliation, particularly since the end of Apartheid. The country excels globally in several major team sports.

The Big Three Major Sports

Three sports dominate the South African sporting landscape in terms of popularity, historical significance, and international success.

1. Rugby Union (The Springboks)

- **Significance**: Rugby holds immense historical and emotional weight. During the Apartheid era, it was primarily supported by the white Afrikaner community.

- **The Change**: The 1995 Rugby World Cup, hosted and won by South Africa, famously featured President Nelson Mandela wearing the jersey of the Springboks (the national team), symbolizing reconciliation and unity.

- **Success**: The Springboks are one of the most successful teams in the world, having won the Rugby World Cup four times (1995, 2007, 2019, 2023).

2. Cricket (The Proteas)

- **Significance**: Cricket has a strong following, particularly among English-speaking white and Indian communities, but enjoys broad support nationally.

- **Teams**: The national team is nicknamed the Proteas. They compete in all three formats of the game: Test matches, One Day Internationals (ODIs), and Twenty20 Internationals (T20Is).

- **History**: After being banned from international cricket during the Apartheid era, South Africa returned to the global stage in 1991. They remain a top-tier international competitor, though they have yet to win a major **International Cricket Council (ICC)** tournament (as of the current date).

3. Football (Soccer - Bafana Bafana)

- **Significance**: Soccer is the most played and widely supported sport among the Black majority population.

- **National Team**: The men's national team is known as Bafana Bafana ("The Boys, The Boys"). The women's team is known as Banyana Banyana.

- **Major Event**: South Africa famously hosted the 2010 FIFA World Cup, becoming the first African nation to do so. The main professional league is the Digital Satellite Television Premiership (previously the **Premier Soccer League (PSL)**).

Other Important Sports

- **Athletics**: South Africa has produced numerous world-class track and field athletes, particularly in middle-distance running, sprinting, and distance events (e.g., Wayde van Niekerk).

- **Golf**: The country has a rich history of success in golf, producing several Major champions, including Gary Player, Ernie Els, and Louis Oosthuizen.

- **Swimming**: South African swimmers have achieved significant Olympic success, most notably since the 2000s (e.g., Chad le Clos and Tatjana Schoenmaker).

- **Marathons and Endurance**: South Africa is famous for hosting two iconic ultra-marathons: the Comrades Marathon (an 89 km race between Durban and Pietermaritzburg) and the Two Oceans Marathon in Cape Town.

Rugby's importance in South Africa is profound, moving far beyond mere sport to become a major political and cultural symbol of division during Apartheid and, subsequently, reconciliation and national unity in the democratic era.

Historical Symbol of Division (Apartheid Era)

For much of the 20th century, the Springboks (the national team) were primarily associated with the white minority, particularly Afrikaner nationalism.

- **Racial Exclusivity**: Until the end of Apartheid, the Springboks were an all-white team. The team's success was often used by the ruling National Party to promote white supremacy and solidify Afrikaner identity.

- **International Isolation**: Due to the government's refusal to allow multiracial sport, the Springboks faced decades of international boycotts and were banned from major competitions, including the first two Rugby World Cups. For Black South Africans, the Springbok emblem was a deeply felt symbol of oppression.

A Force for Reconciliation (Post-1994)

The transition to democracy marked rugby's transformation into a powerful tool for nation-building, largely orchestrated by President Nelson Mandela.

- **The 1995 Rugby World Cup**: This event, hosted and won by South Africa just one year after the first democratic elections, is the single most significant moment in the sport's history.

- o **Mandela's Intervention**: Against the wishes of many in his party who wanted to abolish the Springbok emblem, Mandela adopted it. He met with the predominantly white team and famously attended the final wearing a Springbok jersey with captain Francois Pienaar's number 6.

  - o **Symbolic Unity**: The iconic image of Mandela, the Black president, handing the trophy to Pienaar, the white Afrikaner captain, became a powerful global metaphor for racial reconciliation and the concept of the "Rainbow Nation."

- **Continued Transformation**: Subsequent World Cup victories, notably the 2019 and 2023 wins captained by Siya Kolisi (the Springboks' first Black African captain), continued to symbolize the progress of transformation and shared national pride across all racial lines.

Today, rugby is one of the Big Three major sports, driving patriotism and showcasing South Africa's ability to compete and succeed on the global stage, making it an undeniable cornerstone of the nation's identity.

Chapter 14 — Braaivleis Barbeque

The braai is far more than a way of cooking in South Africa — it is a social ritual, a place where friends, families, and neighbors come together. Whether in a backyard, at a campsite, or overlooking a game reserve, the braai is where stories are shared and connections strengthened. It reflects both the country's outdoor culture and its spirit of hospitality.

This chapter offers a simple look at why the braai remains one of South Africa's most enduring and unifying traditions.

14. Braaivleis Barbeque

Braaivleis (pronounced bry-flays) is an Afrikaans word that literally means "grilled meat" (braai meaning "grill/roast" and vleis meaning "meat").

It is the formal term for the social custom and method of cooking that South Africans universally call a "braai."

A braai is far more than just a casual barbecue; it is a fundamental social ritual and a deeply ingrained part of South African culture that transcends racial and linguistic lines.

Key Differences from a Barbecue

While often compared to a barbecue (BBQ), a braai is distinct in its method and cultural significance.

- **Fuel Source**: A traditional braai is cooked over a wood fire or hot coals (like charcoal or briquettes), not a gas grill. The process of building and tending the fire is considered a key part of the ritual.

- **The "Braai Master"**: There is almost always a designated person, usually a man, who is the "Braai Master." This person is solely responsible for managing the fire, controlling the heat, and cooking the meat to perfection. Others are typically warned not to interfere ("Jy krap nie aan 'n ander man se vuur nie"—*You don't mess with another man's fire*).

- **Social Focus**: A braai is an extended social event that revolves around the fire, not just the food. Guests gather around the fire for hours before, during, and after the meal, sharing drinks and conversation while the cooking happens.

- **The Meat**: While any meat can be used, staples include:

    - *Boerewors*: A traditional spiced farmers' sausage, usually coiled.

    - *Sosaties:* Skewered, marinated meat (often lamb).

    - *Lamb Chops and Steaks.*

The significance is so great that South Africa celebrates its Heritage Day (September 24th) as National Braai Day, symbolizing unity across the diverse "Rainbow Nation."

South African cuisine is a vibrant reflection of its diverse cultures, blending indigenous African traditions with Dutch, Cape Malay, and Indian influences.

Here are some of the most famous and essential foods you should know:

Braai and Meats (The National Obsession)

The Braai (barbecue) is the definitive South African social event, and the meats involved are iconic.

- **Braai/Shisa Nyama**: Not just a meal, but a communal ritual involving grilling meat over an open wood fire. *Shisa Nyama* (Zulu for "burn the meat") refers to the concept of gathering at a butchery or township spot to grill and eat meat.

- **Boerewors**: Literally "farmer's sausage" in Afrikaans. It's a traditional sausage made of minced meat (usually beef, mixed with lamb or pork) spiced heavily with coriander, nutmeg, and cloves, and traditionally coiled into a spiral. It's a staple at any braai.

- **Biltong**: A globally famous South African snack. It is cured, air-dried meat (typically beef or game like kudu or springbok) that is seasoned with vinegar, salt, sugar, and spices, most notably coriander. It differs from jerky by being cured before drying.

Main Dishes & Stews

These dishes represent the country's rich historical fusion:

- **Bobotie**: Often considered South Africa's national dish. It's a baked dish of spiced minced meat (usually beef or lamb) cooked with curry powder, turmeric, and dried fruit (like raisins), topped with an egg and milk custard, and traditionally served with yellow rice. It originated from the Cape Malay community.

- **Bunny Chow**: A quintessential street food originating in Durban's Indian community. It consists of a hollowed-out quarter or half loaf of white bread filled with a hearty curry (usually mutton, chicken, or beans). It's eaten using the bread itself to scoop the curry.

- **Potjiekos**: Meaning "small pot food," this is a traditional stew slow-cooked outdoors in a round, three-legged cast-iron pot (*potjie*) over coals. Ingredients (meat, vegetables, and potatoes) are typically layered and left to simmer without stirring, allowing the flavors to meld separately.

Staples, Sides, and Snacks

- **Pap and Wors**: Pap (pronounced *pup*) is a stiff porridge made from maize meal, similar to polenta or grits, and is a staple carbohydrate for many indigenous groups. It is commonly served with a tomato and onion relish and *wors* (sausage, usually boerewors).

- **Chakalaka**: A colorful, spicy vegetable relish or salad, often made with grated carrots, onions, peppers, and beans, and seasoned with chili and curry powder. It's the perfect zesty side dish for a braai.

- **Vetkoek:** Meaning "fat cake," this is deep-fried yeast dough that resembles a small doughnut (without a hole). It's incredibly versatile, served either savory (stuffed with curried mince) or sweet (dusted with sugar or honey).

A burger and fries would cost about R100

Desserts

- **Malva Pudding**: A rich, sweet, and spongy baked pudding typically made with apricot jam. It is poured over with a hot, creamy caramel sauce immediately after baking, making it sticky and decadent.

- **Melktert (Milk Tart):** A delicate, sweet dessert with a crisp pastry crust and a creamy filling of milk, eggs, and sugar, usually dusted with cinnamon. It has Dutch origins and is a national favorite for tea time.

- **Koeksisters**: The Afrikaner version of a sweet treat. These are plaited (braided) dough pieces that are deep-fried and then immediately plunged into cold, heavy sugar syrup, resulting in a sticky, sweet, and crunchy dessert.

Chapter 15 — Cost of Living – South Africa

The cost of living in South Africa can surprise newcomers — in both directions. Some expenses, like rent and everyday goods, may be far more affordable than in many Western countries, while others, such as electricity, medical care, and insurance, can be unexpectedly high. Understanding these contrasts is essential for anyone considering a move or a long-term stay.

This chapter offers a straightforward look at what daily life truly costs in South Africa, beyond assumptions and quick comparisons.

15. Cost of Living – South Africa

The cost of living in South Africa is generally considered lower than in most major Western countries (like the US, UK, or Western Europe), but it is highly dependent on your lifestyle, and there is significant variation between cities.

Johannesburg, Cape Town, and Durban are the most expensive cities, while smaller towns offer much lower costs.

Here is a breakdown of key cost areas (prices are approximate and subject to exchange rate fluctuations):

1. Housing & Accommodation

Housing is the biggest variable. Renting in major city centers or affluent suburbs is significantly more expensive than anywhere else. 1 US Dollar = approx. 18 Rand, 1 Pound = 23 Rand (November 2025)

Item	Average Monthly Cost (ZAR - South African Rand)	Notes
Rent (1-bed Apt, City Centre)	R 6,500 – R 10,000+	Higher end in wealthy areas like Sandton (JHB) or Camps Bay (CT).
Rent (1-bed Apt, Outside Centre)	R 5,000 – R 7,500	More common in mid-tier suburbs.
Utility Costs (Basic, 1 person)	R 1,500 – R 3,000	Includes electricity, water, garbage, and often high electricity costs due to "load shedding" (power outages).
Internet (Uncapped Fibre)	R 500 – R 1,000	High-speed fibre is widely available and relatively affordable.

2. Food and Groceries

Groceries are generally reasonable, but imported goods are expensive. Eating out can be quite affordable compared to international prices.

Item	Estimated Cost (ZAR)	Notes
Milk (1 liter)	R 18 – R 25	Standard price.
Loaf of Bread (White)	R 15 – R 20	Basic necessity price.
Dozen Eggs	R 35 – R 50	Price fluctuates.
Mid-Range Restaurant Meal	R 150 – R 300 per person	Excluding drinks; depends heavily on the establishment.
Local Beer (0.5 liter draft) at a bar or restaurant	R 35 – R 50	Affordable.
Bottle of Mid-Range Wine	R 80 – R 150	Wine is excellent value due to local production.

3. Transportation

While public transport options exist (like the Gautrain in Gauteng), most South Africans rely on private transport, making car-related costs important.

Item	Estimated Cost (ZAR)	Notes
Gasoline (1 liter)	R 23 – R 26+	Fluctuates frequently due to global oil prices and taxes.
Monthly Public Transport Pass	R 500 – R 1,000	Varies heavily; primarily applicable to the Gautrain or municipal buses.
Taxi/Uber (per km)	R 8 – R 12	Uber/e-hailing services are very popular and widely used.

4. Overall Monthly Estimate (Single Person)

Excluding rent, a single person living a moderate lifestyle might spend approximately R 9,000 to R 15,000 per month on living expenses.

Key Takeaways for Cost of Living

- **Service vs. Goods**: Local services (eating out, domestic help, local travel) are generally cheaper. Imported goods (electronics, luxury clothing) are often as expensive as or more expensive than in Western countries.

- **Security Costs**: Many people living in suburbs factor in additional monthly costs for private security, alarm systems, and armed response (ranging from R 500 to R 2,000+) due to high crime rates.

Housing Estate Johannesburg – Townhouse

Chapter 16 — Crime and Security

Crime is a reality in South Africa, and understanding it clearly is essential for anyone living in or visiting the country. The risks are real, but so are the strategies people use every day to stay safe and navigate their surroundings with confidence. South Africans themselves are resilient, adaptable, and often remarkably resourceful when it comes to personal security.

This chapter offers a practical, level-headed look at crime and safety — not to instill fear, but to provide the knowledge needed to move about wisely and well-prepared.

16. Crime and Security

Both security and crime are significant issues in South Africa, and they are major factors that both residents and visitors must be aware of and actively manage. I think the best advice I can give is to drive when you can unless it is safe to walk such as in the suburbs, but you should be aware of your surrounding and where you are. Gyms are quite popular such as Virgin Active or Planet Fitness but require a contract to join. Do not carry a lot of cash, and avoid taking your phone in dangerous areas/or at night. I guess like certain places in New York. Be Streetwise. Drive when you can and walk when it is safe. Be aware of your surroundings, not to be paranoid but to know the country.

The country has high rates of both violent and non-violent crimes, though the risk is highly concentrated in certain areas and mitigated by common safety practices.

Key Security Challenges

1. High Rates of Violent Crime

South Africa has one of the highest per capita rates of violent crime globally.

- **Murder and Assault**: High murder rates, often linked to gang activity, poverty, and social issues, are a persistent national crisis.

- **Sexual Offenses**: The country also faces extremely high rates of sexual assault and gender-based violence, which are critical social and security concerns.

2. Property and Non-Violent Crime

Crimes targeting property and possessions are very common, particularly in urban areas.

- **Robbery and Mugging**: Street robberies are common, particularly in crowded city centers or near transport hubs.

- **House Break-ins and Carjacking**: Residential break-ins and hijackings (car theft involving force) are frequent occurrences, leading many residents to live in security complexes or suburbs with high walls, electric fences, and armed response services.

Mitigation and Management for Residents & Visitors

Security is often a managed risk in South Africa, meaning that safety is largely achieved through awareness and preventative measures.

- **Residential Security**: Most middle and upper-income homes and complexes employ high-level security measures, including alarm systems, armed response subscriptions, electric fences, and security gates.

- **Avoid High-Risk Areas**: Townships and informal settlements generally have higher crime rates and should be entered only with a local guide or tour operator. Avoid walking alone at night in city centers or isolated areas.

- **Driving Safety**: Always keep car doors locked and windows rolled up, especially when stopped at traffic lights. When parking, choose secure, well-lit parking lots.

- **Be Discreet**: Avoid openly displaying wealth, such as expensive jewelry, cameras, or smartphones, in public areas, as this can make you a target for opportunistic crime.

- **Use Reputable Transport**: Rely on reputable taxi services, ride-sharing apps (like Uber/Bolt), or secured transport organized by hotels rather than unmarked street taxis.

While the crime statistics are sobering, most major tourist destinations (like the immediate areas around Table Mountain, major shopping malls, and dedicated wine routes) are generally safe, provided visitors adhere to standard urban safety protocols.

Safety on public transport in South Africa is a complex issue; while millions use it daily without incident, it is generally considered a significant concern, especially on certain types of transport and routes. Safety varies dramatically depending on the city, the time of day, and the specific mode of transport used.

Safety by Transport Type

1. E-hailing Services (Uber/Bolt) & Taxis

- **Safety Level**: Generally High (Best Option for Visitors)

- **Notes**: E-hailing services are very popular, reliable, and generally the safest and most recommended option for tourists and residents in urban areas. Services track the journey and driver details are verified. Reputable metered taxis are also reliable.

2. Gautrain (Gauteng only)

- **Safety Level**: Excellent

- **Notes**: The Gautrain (linking Johannesburg, Pretoria, and O.R. Tambo International Airport) is a modern, clean, and highly secure commuter rail service. It is considered very safe due to constant surveillance and dedicated security personnel.

3. Rea Vaya/MyCiTi Buses (BRT Systems)

- **Safety Level**: Good

- **Notes**: These are Bus Rapid Transit (BRT) systems in Johannesburg and Cape Town, respectively. They operate on dedicated routes, use centralized ticketing, and are generally well-managed and safe, comparable to public transit systems in many major world cities.

4. Passenger Rail Agency of South Africa (PRASA) / Metrorail

- **Safety Level:** Low/High Risk

- **Notes**: The suburban and long-distance commuter rail networks (Metrorail) are often plagued by issues. Trains are frequently late, overcrowded, and subject to vandalism, theft, and occasional violence, particularly during off-peak hours or late at night. This option is generally not recommended for tourists or inexperienced commuters.

5. Minibus Taxis (Informal)

- **Safety Level**: Low

- **Notes**: These privately owned 10-15 seater vans form the backbone of public transport for the majority of the working population. They are generally unregulated and unsafe in terms of driving standards (overcrowding, speeding, reckless driving) and carry a risk of petty crime. Avoid using them unless you are very familiar with the route and culture.

Safety Advice for Public Transport

To minimize risk, you should follow standard safety precautions:

- **Avoid Travelling on public transport at Night unless driving**: Crime risks increase significantly after dark, especially on trains and in isolated areas.

- **Do Not Display Valuables**: Keep phones, cash, and jewelry out of sight, especially near windows or doors.

- **Travel with Company:** If using trains or buses, traveling in a group is always safer.

- **Use Recommended Services**: For visiting, stick to the e-hailing services (Uber/Bolt) and the modern BRT bus systems where available.

Poverty and Crime

Poverty and crime in South Africa are deeply intertwined and driven by a complex legacy of extreme inequality stemming from the apartheid era. Research consistently points to a strong correlation, particularly in marginalized communities.

The Core Relationship: Inequality as the Super-Driver

While poverty itself is a factor, the primary driver linking economic conditions to crime in South Africa is Income and Spatial Inequality.

- **Relative Deprivation**: South Africa has one of the highest Gini coefficients (a measure of inequality) globally. The stark, visible gap between wealthy and impoverished areas—often bordering one another due to historical spatial segregation—fosters intense social tension, resentment, and frustration. This feeling of relative deprivation is a major catalyst for both property and violent crime.

- **Survivalist Crime**: High rates of unemployment, especially youth unemployment (which can be over 60% in some areas), limit legitimate economic opportunities. This pushes many into "survivalist crimes" like theft, burglary, and robbery as a means of generating much-needed income.

- **Economic Opportunity**: Criminal activities, particularly property crimes, are often seen as high-return, low-risk ventures compared to low-paying or non-existent formal employment, aligning with economic theories of crime.

Key Socio-Economic Factors Fueling Crime

Crime in South Africa is not solely an economic issue; it is a systemic problem rooted in multiple overlapping failures:

- **High Unemployment**: The lack of formal jobs, particularly for young people, is consistently cited as a direct contributor to criminality, gang activity, and social breakdown.

- **Historical Legacy of Apartheid**: Systemic marginalization and racial segregation created deep, enduring structural problems, including unequal access to quality education, housing, and infrastructure, which still predict crime prevalence today. That said, many white people are also struggling because of laws which favour Black, Coloured and Asian people with the laws surrounding BEE (Black Economic Empowerment), and B-BBEE (Broad-Based Black Economic Empowerment).

- **Substance Abuse**: High levels of alcohol and drug abuse are strongly linked to the commission of many violent crimes, including murder, assault, and gender-based violence.

- **Normalization of Violence**: Decades of political and social violence have contributed to a culture where violence is often seen as a legitimate or necessary means of conflict resolution or asserting power (especially within a highly patriarchal social context).

- **Weak Rule of Law:** Inefficiency, corruption, and a lack of resources within the police and criminal justice system lead to a perception of impunity, further emboldening criminal elements.

The Impact of Crime on Development

The high crime rate also perpetuates the cycle of poverty and underdevelopment.

- **Economic Cost**: Crime is estimated to cost the South African economy a substantial percentage of its Gross Domestic Product (GDP) annually through stolen property, protection costs (security services, insurance), and lost investment.

- **Deterred Investment**: High crime, particularly organized crime (like illegal mining or infrastructure theft), discourages foreign direct investment and stifles long-term economic growth.

- **Social Breakdown:** Crime erodes social cohesion and public trust, forcing households and businesses to invest heavily in private security, further exacerbating the visible divide between the secure wealthy and the vulnerable poor.

Gym in South Africa — Planet Fitness North Johannesburg
Common gyms in South Africa include Virgin Active and Planet Fitness, and you can get memberships for specific gyms, or areas, or around the country.
Normally you need to get a one year membership.

Virgin Active membership costs in South Africa vary significantly based on the type of membership, club location, and current promotions.

Here is an approximate breakdown of costs, with the important reminder to always confirm the exact price with the specific club you plan to join, as prices can differ widely across the country.

1. Monthly Membership Fees (Approximate Ranges)

Membership Type	Target Access	Typical Monthly Cost Range (ZAR)	Key Features
Club (Off-Peak)	Single Club, Restricted Hours (e.g., no weekday evenings)	R450 – R1,070	Lower cost, single club, time restrictions.
Club (Full Access)	Single Club, Unrestricted Hours	R550 – R1,370	Full-day access at one club.
Premier	Multi-Club Access (excluding Collection Clubs)	R790 – R1,570	Access to over 130 clubs nationwide.
Collection	Premium/Exclusive Clubs + all other clubs	R2,900 – R4,200	Access to high-end Collection clubs and all other clubs.

Membership Type	Target Access	Typical Monthly Cost Range (ZAR)	Key Features
Youth Premier (Ages 14-17)	Multi-Club Access	R450 – R500	Discounted rate for younger teens.
Youth Premier (Ages 18-23)	Multi-Club Access	R950 – R1,000	Discounted rate for older youth/students.
Kids (Under 14)	Club-V/Club-V Max	Around R155	Membership for the child facilities.

- **Location Impact**: A Club Off-Peak membership in a smaller town might be around R450/month, while a Premier or Collection membership in a major metropolitan club (like Melrose Arch, Johannesburg) can cost up to R3,400/month or more.

- **Contract Length**: Signing up for a 24-month contract is typically cheaper per month than a 12-month or month-to-month option.

2. Joining and Other Fees

- **Joining Fee**: This can vary, but is often around R399 for Club memberships. For Premier or Collection memberships, it can sometimes be equal to one month's full retail rate.

- **Access Card/Band Fee**: A small, additional fee may apply for your access device.

- **Promotions:** Virgin Active frequently runs campaigns that offer discounted or waived joining fees and other benefits like the first month free or a percentage off the monthly fee for a period.

3. Discounts and Medical Aid Partners

A large number of South African members use medical aid partners for significant discounts:

- **Discovery Vitality:** Offers up to 75% off monthly fees, depending on your plan and Vitality status/points.

- **Momentum Multiply**: Offers savings, often around 25% off monthly fees.

Your best next step is to visit the Virgin Active South Africa website or call your nearest club directly. They will be able to give you the most accurate and current pricing based on the exact club and membership tier you are interested in.

Chapter 17 — Driving in South Africa

Driving in South Africa can be both rewarding and challenging. The country offers long open roads, breathtaking scenery, and well-traveled routes — but it also demands awareness, patience, and a clear understanding of local conditions. Traffic patterns, road quality, and regional differences can vary widely from place to place.

This chapter provides a practical guide to what drivers can expect, helping newcomers navigate the roads with confidence and realistic expectations.

17. Driving in South Africa

This is the safest option in South Africa is driving by car even at night. Carrying the correct items in your car in South Africa is essential for both legal compliance and personal safety and readiness, especially given the unique challenges of long distances, extreme heat, and security concerns.

Here is a comprehensive breakdown of what you should carry, categorized by importance.

1. Mandatory & Legal Documents

You must have the following documents readily available in the car at all times to comply with the National Road Traffic Act:

- **Driver's License**: Your valid physical driver's license. If you are a foreigner, carry your original foreign license and an International Driving Permit (IDP) if your license is not in English.

- **Proof of Registration**: Documentation proving the vehicle is legally registered (the license disk should be visibly displayed on the windscreen).

- **Vehicle Insurance**: While not always legally mandatory to carry the policy itself, having proof of third-party liability insurance is highly recommended in case of an accident.

2. Safety & Breakdown Essentials (Legal & Best Practice)

These items are crucial for roadside emergencies, and some are legally required:

Item	Importance & Notes
Reflective Warning Triangle	Legally Mandatory. Must be used to warn oncoming traffic if you break down, especially on highways. Many drivers carry two or three for better visibility.
Spare Tyre (in good condition)	Legally Mandatory. Must be correctly inflated and accessible.
Jack and Wheel Spanner	Tools required to change a tyre. Always ensure they are present and in working order.
First Aid Kit	Highly Recommended. Essential for rendering aid. Stock it with plasters, antiseptic wipes, pain relievers, and gauze.
Jumper Cables	Essential for battery failures, which are common.
Flashlight / Torch	Essential. Needed for breakdowns, especially at night or during power outages (*load shedding*). Ideally, one that can be charged via the car.

3. Personal Safety & Security

Given the security risks in urban and remote areas, these items are wise additions:

- **Emergency Contact Info**: A physical card with emergency numbers

    - Police: 10111,
    - Ambulance: 10177,
    - Roadside Assistance.

- **Emergency Cash**: A small amount of cash (e.g., R100-R500) for tolls, small purchases, or emergencies when ATMs are unavailable or risky to use.

- **Backup Phone Charger**: A dedicated car charger or power bank to ensure your phone never runs flat, especially in remote areas.

- **Torch/Spare light** in case of breakdowns.

- **Spare/Hidden Phone**: Some residents carry a basic, charged, hidden phone for use in case their primary smartphone is stolen during a *smash-and-grab* or hijacking.

- **Do Not Leave Valuables in Sight**: While not carried *in* the car, remember to keep phones, bags, cameras, and purses out of sight or locked in the boot (trunk) when driving or parking.

4. Comfort & Long-Distance Driving

South African road trips can be long and hot, making these items vital:

- **Water**: At least 2 litres of fresh water per person, as high temperatures can lead to dehydration or engine overheating.

- **Non-Perishable Snacks**: Energy bars, nuts, or crackers in case of unexpected delays.

- **Road Maps**: A physical map or offline GPS downloads in case cellphone signal is lost in remote areas.

- **Coolant/Oil**: A spare bottle of engine coolant and a small bottle of engine oil, especially for long drives.

*Stuck in **Port St. John's** after driving through the night.
This was the last time I tried to drive through the Transkei
at night. Got 2 flat tyres after hitting unmarked speed bumps
at 80 – 100 km/hour near Flagstaff, Transkei, off the N2.*

Driving through the Transkei

On the N3

N3 to Durban

Chapter 18 — Being Safe While Travelling

Travelling through South Africa can be an unforgettable experience, but it requires a bit of preparation and common sense. Most journeys are pleasant and trouble-free, yet being aware of your surroundings and understanding local travel patterns make a meaningful difference. South Africans themselves travel widely and confidently, using simple habits that help keep them safe on the road, at airports, and in unfamiliar areas.

This chapter outlines practical tips for staying secure while traveling, so you can focus on the beauty and diversity the country has to offer.

18. Being safe while Travelling

Staying prepared is key to safe driving in South Africa. If you are renting a car, always confirm that the spare tyre, jack, and reflective triangle are present and in good condition before driving off. Pot holes are common on roads, due to corruption and roads not being fixed. Most National roads like the N1, N2, and N3 are good roads.

The "best" way to travel in South Africa depends entirely on your budget, time constraints, destination type, and desire for independence.

South Africa is vast, and a single method of transport won't cover every scenario. The best approach is usually a combination of methods.

Here is a breakdown of the best options for different travel needs:

1. Domestic Flights (For Long Distances & Time Savings)

If you need to cover large distances quickly (e.g., Johannesburg to Cape Town, which is a 14-16 hour drive), flying is highly recommended.

- **Pros:** Fastest, safest, and most convenient for covering the country's huge distances.

- **Cons**: Less scenic, and you miss out on the places in between. You still need transport from the airport.

- **Airlines**: Reliable low-cost carriers include FlySafair and Airlink (which services smaller, regional airports like those near Kruger National Park). SAA (South African Airways) is the flag carrier.

2. Self-Drive/Car Rental (For Flexibility & Scenery)

This is the most popular and highly recommended method for independent travelers, especially for specific routes like the Garden Route, the Winelands, or safaris in the Kruger National Park.

- **Pros**: Maximum flexibility, allowing you to stop when and where you want. Roads between major cities and tourist areas are generally excellent and well-signposted.

- **Cons**: Long driving distances are involved. Security requires vigilance (car doors locked, valuables out of sight). You must avoid driving at night, especially in unfamiliar areas.

- **Best For**: Road trips, wine tours, and safaris (a 2WD sedan is usually sufficient for main roads in most parks, including Kruger).

3. Modern Urban Public Transport (For City Travel)

In major cities, a few systems are reliable and safe:

- **E-hailing/Ride-sharing (Uber/Bolt):** The most common, convenient, and safest way to get around in all major cities (Cape Town, Johannesburg, Durban). Use these, particularly at night. They can be expensive though and you should avoid drinking and driving because there are road blocks. One Uber Fair could cover renting a car for the day depending upon distance, but if drinking, go for the ride sharing app.

- **Gautrain (Gauteng):** An excellent, fast, efficient, and highly secure express train linking O.R. Tambo Airport (JNB) with Johannesburg suburbs (Sandton) and Pretoria. Highly recommended for airport transfers.

- **MyCiTi/Rea Vaya Buses (Cape Town/Johannesburg):** These Bus Rapid Transit (BRT) systems are modern, safe, and reliable for daytime travel on their dedicated routes.

4. Long-Distance Buses & Shuttles (Budget-Friendly)

For budget-conscious travelers who do not want to drive, reputable inter-city coach companies are a good alternative.

- **Coach Companies**: Intercape, Greyhound, and Translux offer comfortable, safe, and affordable connections between major cities.

- **Backpacker Buses**: The Baz Bus operates a hop-on, hop-off service along popular backpacker routes (like the Garden Route), which is a sociable option.

Transport to Generally Avoid

For safety and reliability reasons, foreign visitors are generally advised to avoid:

- **Minibus Taxis**: The ubiquitous, privately-owned vans that form the public transport backbone. They are cheap but follow chaotic, non-fixed schedules and carry higher security and driving risks.

- **Metrorail/Commuter Trains**: The standard commuter rail system (outside of the Gautrain) is often unreliable, subject to theft and vandalism, and generally unsafe.

In summary, the best travel combination is to Fly between major hubs and Rent a Car for regional sightseeing and road trips, using Uber/Bolt within the cities.

Along the Indian Ocean coastline — a quiet stretch of beachfront.

Chapter 19 — South African Women

The story of South Africa cannot be told without acknowledging the strength and resilience of its women. Across cultures and provinces, South African women hold families together, lead communities, and navigate challenges with determination shaped by both history and daily realities. Their roles are diverse — from professionals and entrepreneurs to caregivers and activists — yet they share a common thread of perseverance.

This chapter offers a look at the experiences, contributions, and leadership of women in South Africa today.

19. South African Women

South African women have a complex, powerful, and often contradictory status in the country's history and modern society. They are celebrated for their monumental role in the fight against Apartheid, yet they still grapple with severe issues of gender inequality and violence.

Here is a summary of their importance and status:

1. Legacy of Resistance and Liberation

South African women were central figures in the fight for freedom and equality.

- **The 1956 Women's March**: This is the defining moment. On August 9, 1956, over 20,000 women of all races marched to the Union Buildings in Pretoria to protest the extension of the dehumanizing Pass Laws to women. This date is now celebrated as National Women's Day in South Africa.

- **Key Icons**: Women like Albertina Sisulu, Lillian Ngoyi, and Helen Joseph, were the vanguard of the anti-Apartheid movement, facing detention, exile, and torture.

- **Foundation for Rights:** Their struggle ensured that South Africa's post-1994 Constitution became one of the world's most progressive documents, specifically guaranteeing non-discrimination based on race and gender.

2. Visible Presence in Politics and Business

South African women are highly visible in public and corporate life, often exceeding global averages in senior roles.

- **Political Representation**: Women consistently hold a high proportion of seats in the National Parliament (around 46% as of 2024), placing South Africa well above the global average.

- **Inspirational Leaders**: Women like Professor Thuli Madonsela (former Public Protector who championed good governance), Nicky Newton-King (first woman to run the Johannesburg Stock Exchange - JSE), and the late singer Miriam Makeba ("Mama Africa," a Grammy winner and activist) are internationally recognized figures.

- **Business Leadership**: South African women hold a significant number of senior management roles (nearly 47% in mid-market companies), even surpassing global averages in roles like CFO and HR Officer.

3. Persistent Challenges: Gender-Based Violence (GBV)

Despite progressive laws and political representation, the most significant issue facing women in South Africa is the alarmingly high rate of gender-based violence (GBV) and femicide.

- **High Femicide Rate:** South Africa's femicide rate is several times the global average, leading many to describe the situation as a national crisis or a "shadow pandemic."

- **Intimate Partner Violence**: A large percentage of women report having experienced physical and/or sexual violence by an intimate partner.

- **Unpaid Care Work:** Women still disproportionately bear the burden of unpaid care and domestic work, which limits their economic and educational opportunities, particularly in rural and poorer communities.

Summary

South African women are defined by their resilience, political strength, and cultural diversity. They are the keepers of families and traditions, the drivers of significant economic sectors, and have secured world-leading rights on paper. However, the daily struggle against violence and entrenched socio-economic inequality remains the primary challenge to achieving full gender justice.

Chapter 20 — South African Men

South African men come from many backgrounds, cultures, and histories, yet they share a landscape that has shaped their identities in powerful ways. Whether living in cities, townships, or rural provinces, they navigate expectations influenced by tradition, work, family life, and the country's complex past. Their experiences vary widely, but together they form an essential part of South Africa's social fabric. This chapter offers a grounded look at the lives, roles, and responsibilities of men across the country today.

20. South African Men

South African men, much like the entire country, are defined by incredible diversity across culture, ethnicity, language, and socio-economic background.

It's impossible to talk about a single "South African man" because their experiences are shaped by their specific identity.

Here are some key aspects to consider:

Diversity and Identity

- **Multiculturalism**: South Africa is known as the "Rainbow Nation," and its male population reflects this. Men belong to various groups, including:

    - **Black Africans**: Comprising the majority, with diverse ethnic groups like Zulu, Xhosa, Sotho, Tswana, Pedi, and more, each with their own rich cultural traditions and languages.

    - **Coloureds**: A multi-ethnic group with roots in indigenous, African, European, and Asian ancestry.

    - **White South Africans**: Primarily divided into Afrikaners (descended from Dutch, German, and French settlers, speaking Afrikaans) and English-speakers (descended from British and other European groups).

- o **Indian/Asian**: Descendants of indentured laborers and traders, mainly concentrated in KwaZulu-Natal.

- **Post-Apartheid Generation**: Younger generations are growing up in a democratic South Africa with different social and economic challenges and opportunities than their fathers, leading to new ways of defining masculinity.

- **Urban vs. Rural**: The life of a man in a bustling city like Johannesburg or Cape Town is vastly different from one living in a traditional rural village in the Eastern Cape or Limpopo.

Culture and Tradition

- **Traditional Masculinities**: Many indigenous cultures have formal processes for transitioning from boyhood to manhood, such as the Xhosa tradition of ulwaluko (initiation/circumcision), which imparts moral and community values. These traditions often emphasize discipline, respect, and responsibility.

- **Ubuntu**: A concept prominent among many Black South African cultures, often translated as "humanity" or "I am because we are." It emphasizes compassion, reciprocity, and the interconnectedness of people. Men are often expected to embody this spirit in their communities and families.

- **Braai Culture**: A very popular and unifying social tradition across all cultural groups is the braai (barbecue), where men often take a lead role in preparing and cooking the meat.

Modern Roles and Challenges

- **Gender Roles**: While traditional expectations often place men as the head of the household and primary provider, South Africa is undergoing significant shifts. In urban and modern families, many men and women share financial and household responsibilities, though there are still significant public discussions and challenges regarding outdated patriarchal attitudes.

- **Socio-Economic Issues**: South African men face high rates of unemployment, poverty, and inequality, which can put immense pressure on traditional roles as providers.

- **Activism**: There are ongoing national conversations and campaigns, often involving men's health and the fight against gender-based violence (GBV), which is a serious societal problem. For example, events like the Hollard Daredevil Run raise awareness for male cancers.

Ultimately, a South African man can be a traditional Zulu chief, an Afrikaner entrepreneur, a "coloured" artist from the Cape Flats, a Xhosa banker in Sandton, or an Indian shopkeeper in Durban—each one a unique thread in the nation's diverse fabric.

Chapter 21 — Corruption within the ANC

South Africa's modern challenges cannot be understood without acknowledging the impact of corruption within the African National Congress (ANC). Once the party that carried the hopes of a newly democratic nation, the ANC has in recent decades faced scandals, mismanagement, and internal divisions that have weakened public trust and strained essential institutions. These issues affect everything from service delivery to economic growth and daily life for ordinary citizens.

This chapter looks at how corruption developed within the party, and what it has meant for the country's progress.

21. Corruption within the ANC

Corruption in South Africa, particularly within the ruling African National Congress (ANC), is widely acknowledged as one of the country's most significant and debilitating challenges since the end of Apartheid. It ranges from petty bribery to sophisticated, large-scale looting of state resources especially under the Zuma presidency.

The ANC and Systemic Corruption

While the ANC was the liberation movement that brought democracy, the party has been at the center of the country's biggest corruption scandals over the past three decades.

1. The Arms Deal Scandal (Late 1990s)

- **What it was**: A massive purchase of military equipment from European companies shortly after the end of Apartheid.

- **Significance:** This was the first major post-1994 scandal, leading to persistent allegations of bribery and fraud involving high-ranking ANC officials, including former President Jacob Zuma, and setting a precedent for questionable public procurement.

2. State Capture (The Zuma Era, 2009–2018)

This is the most destructive form of corruption to affect democratic South Africa.

- **Definition**: State Capture is a form of systemic political corruption where private interests (notably the powerful Gupta family) illicitly exert control over the state's decision-making process, including cabinet appointments, policy, and the management of State-Owned Enterprises (SOEs), to benefit themselves financially.

- **The Zondo Commission**: A judicial commission of inquiry (the Zondo Commission) spent years investigating these allegations. Its final report detailed how the ANC, under the leadership of Jacob Zuma, allegedly "permitted, supported and enabled corruption" that cost the country hundreds of billions of Rands.

- **Key SOEs Affected**: Entities like Eskom (the national power utility), Transnet (rail and port freight), and SAA (South African Airways) were systematically weakened and plundered, directly contributing to South Africa's current economic crises and infrastructure failures (like ongoing power outages, known as *load shedding*).

3. Corruption Within Policy Frameworks

Policies designed to address historical inequality have sometimes been exploited:

- **Black Economic Empowerment (BEE):** While intended to economically empower historically disadvantaged groups, the policy has, at times, been manipulated through tender fraud and *BEE fronting* (where qualifying individuals are used as tokens) to funnel government contracts and resources to politically connected individuals ("tenderpreneurs").

Corruption in South Africa Generally

Corruption is not confined to the top tiers of the ANC; it permeates various levels of public life:

- **Petty Corruption:** This involves small-scale bribery or illicit payments in daily life, such as police officers soliciting bribes, or minor payments to officials to speed up public services (like obtaining licenses or permits).

- **COVID-19 PPE Fraud**: The pandemic exposed massive corruption, with reports of widespread looting and inflated prices for essential Personal Protective Equipment (PPE) by politically connected individuals and companies.

- **International Perception**: Transparency International's Corruption Perceptions Index (CPI) consistently scores South Africa below the global average (the score has generally stagnated or slightly declined over recent years), indicating persistent high levels of public sector corruption. In the 2024 CPI (assessing 2023), South Africa scored 41/100 (where 100 is very clean).

Current Efforts

Under President Cyril Ramaphosa, there has been a stated focus on fighting corruption, although he has also been implicated, largely through implementing the recommendations of the Zondo Commission. Efforts include strengthening institutions like the National Prosecuting Authority (NPA) and the establishment of dedicated anti-corruption units, though many critics argue that the pace of arrests and prosecutions remains too slow.

Madlanga Commission (2025)

The commission currently operating in South Africa, which is investigating allegations made by KwaZulu-Natal Police Commissioner Lieutenant-General Nhlanhla Mkhwanazi, is formally known as the Judicial Commission of Inquiry into Criminality, Political Interference, and Corruption in the Criminal Justice System.

It is most commonly referred to as the Madlanga Commission, after its chairperson, retired acting Deputy Chief Justice Mbuyiseli Madlanga.

The commission was established following the allegations made by General Mkhwanazi, here is the information:

The Madlanga Commission (*Prompted by Mkhwanazi's Allegations*)

Purpose and Background

- **Trigger**: The commission was established by President Cyril Ramaphosa in July 2025 following serious public allegations made by KZN Police Commissioner Lt Gen Nhlanhla Mkhwanazi.

- **Mkhwanazi's Allegations**: General Mkhwanazi publicly alleged that South Africa's criminal justice and law enforcement system [including the South African Police Service (SAPS), the National Prosecuting Authority (NPA), and intelligence services] had been infiltrated by sophisticated criminal syndicates and subjected to political interference.

- **Key Focus Areas**: The commission is tasked with investigating:

- o The role of organized crime and criminal syndicates in law enforcement institutions.

- o Allegations of political interference in sensitive police investigations (such as the disbandment of the Political Killings Task Team in KZN).

- o Whether current or former senior government officials or members of the National Executive were complicit in, or benefited from, this corruption.

Significance

- The establishment of this commission indicates the severity of the allegations, suggesting that corruption in South Africa has moved beyond mere *State Capture* by private business interests (as investigated by the Zondo Commission) to involve potential capture by violent criminal cartels directly undermining public safety and the rule of law.

- The commission has heard testimony from high-ranking officials and has begun to detail the mechanisms of interference, including the use of high-level connections to manipulate investigations and suppress justice.

Mkhwanazi, is the police general whose explosive revelations led to the inquiry's establishment.

Farmgate Scandal

This is a crucial issue, as it hits at the very heart of the anti-corruption platform on which President Ramaphosa was elected. The scandal is widely known as the "Phala Phala" or "Farmgate" scandal.

Here is a summary of the complex allegations and developments surrounding the controversy:

The Phala Phala Scandal (Farmgate)

The scandal revolves around a robbery that occurred in February 2020 at President Cyril Ramaphosa's private Phala Phala game farm in Limpopo province.

The Core Allegations

1. **The Theft of Cash**: An indeterminate amount of U.S. dollars in cash was allegedly stolen from the farm. The President confirmed the robbery but stated the money was a much lower figure than what was reported by the accuser—the proceeds from the sale of game animals (buffaloes).

   o **The Accusation**: The complaint, lodged in June 2022 by former State Security Agency boss Arthur Fraser (a known political rival), alleged that millions of dollars (reported as high as $4 million) were hidden in furniture (specifically, a couch) on the farm.

- o **Ramaphosa's Claim**: The President stated the amount was significantly less (around $580,000) and that it was derived from legitimate sales of his cattle and game.

2. **Failure to Report and Cover-Up**: The central accusation is that the President failed to officially report the crime to the South African Police Service (SAPS) and the South African Revenue Service (SARS) to avoid scrutiny over the source of the foreign currency.

   - o Fraser alleged that Ramaphosa had instead used his Presidential Protection Unit to secretly track down the suspects (who were Namibian citizens and South Africans) and recover the cash, which would constitute an abuse of power and a cover-up.

   - o Ramaphosa admitted reporting the incident to the head of his protection unit, which falls under SAPS, but critics argue this was an improper channel.

3. **Money Laundering/Currency Laws**: Questions were raised about why a large amount of foreign currency was kept in cash on the property, and whether the money was properly declared to the Reserve Bank and tax authorities, potentially breaching South Africa's currency control laws.

Investigations and Political Fallout

The scandal led to several political and legal inquiries:

- **Parliamentary Independent Panel:** Parliament established an independent panel, which concluded in late 2022 that President Ramaphosa "may have committed" serious violations of the Constitution and misconduct. This triggered a vote in Parliament on whether to initiate formal impeachment proceedings.

- **Parliamentary Vote**: The ANC leadership instructed its Members of Parliament (MPs) to vote against the adoption of the panel's report. Ramaphosa narrowly survived the motion to initiate impeachment proceedings.

- **Public Protector (Anti-Corruption Watchdog):** South Africa's anti-corruption ombudswoman, the Public Protector, conducted an investigation and in mid-2023, found no evidence that President Ramaphosa violated the Executive Ethics Code or exposed himself to a conflict of interest. (However, the police investigation into the robbery and related crimes continued).

- **Ongoing Criminal Investigation:** The Directorate for Priority Crime Investigation (Hawks), the elite police unit, is conducting an investigation into the allegations lodged by Arthur Fraser.

- **Trial of Robbery Suspects:** A separate criminal trial against the individuals accused of carrying out the theft at the farm has been proceeding in the regional court.

Why It Matters

Ramaphosa came to power in 2018 on a mandate to clean up the widespread "state capture" and corruption that occurred under his predecessor, Jacob Zuma. The Phala Phala scandal seriously undermined his anti-corruption credibility and became a rallying point for both opposition parties and political rivals within his own party, the African National Congress (ANC).

Solar panels Northgate shopping center – April 2025

Solar-powered LED grip lights — popular essentials for coping with load shedding and ensuring safety during travel.

Chapter 22 — Visas to South Africa

Understanding South Africa's visa requirements is an important step for anyone considering travel, work, or long-term residence in the country. The system is generally straightforward, but it includes several categories that depend on a visitor's purpose, length of stay, and professional background. Knowing what documents are needed — and how timelines can vary — helps avoid unnecessary delays or frustration.

This chapter offers a simple, practical guide to the most common visa options and what newcomers should expect.

22. Visas to South Africa

Visa requirements for South Africa depend entirely on your nationality, the purpose of your visit, and the intended duration of your stay.

South Africa's visa system is categorized into short-term Visitor's Visas and various Temporary Residence Visas for longer stays or specific purposes.

1. Visa Exemptions (Port of Entry Visa)

Citizens of many countries (including the US, UK, Canada, Australia, and most Western European nations) do not require a visa for short tourist or business visits.

- **Duration**: Typically, these visitors are granted a Visitor's Permit upon arrival at a South African port of entry (like an airport), which is usually valid for 90 days or less.

- **Key Requirement**: Even if you are visa-exempt, you must have:

    - A passport valid for no less than 30 days after your intended date of departure.

    - At least two unused, blank pages in your passport for entry/departure stamps.

    - Proof of a return or onward ticket.

2. Visitor's Visa (For Visa-Required Nationalities)

If your country is not on the visa-exempt list, you must apply for a Visitor's Visa at a South African embassy, consulate, or designated application center (like VFS Global) in your country *before* you travel. Visas are not issued at the port of entry.

General Requirements for Application:

- Completed application form (DHA-84).

- Valid passport (meeting the criteria above).

- Two recent identical passport photographs.

- Proof of sufficient funds (e.g., recent bank statements for the last three months).

- Documentation confirming the purpose and duration of the visit (e.g., hotel reservations, itinerary, or a letter of invitation from a host).

- Proof of accommodation.

- Payment of the prescribed, non-refundable application fee.

3. Temporary Residence Visas (For Longer or Specific Stays)

If your intended stay is longer than 90 days or if the purpose is not tourism, you must apply for a specific Temporary Residence Visa (TRV) before entering South Africa. Common types include:

Visa Type	Purpose	Notes
Study Visa	For students enrolled in a South African educational institution.	Requires an official acceptance letter and proof of medical insurance.
General Work Visa	For foreigners with an employer-specific job offer in South Africa.	Requires proof that the employer attempted to hire a South African citizen first.
Critical Skills Work Visa	For applicants with skills identified as scarce in South Africa.	Often allows entry without a prior job offer, based on qualifications.
Business Visa	For establishing or investing in a business in South Africa.	Requires detailed business plans and proof of investment funds.
Retired Person's Visa	For foreigners intending to retire in South Africa.	Requires proof of guaranteed lifelong income or net worth.

Visa Type	Purpose	Notes
Digital Nomad/Remote Work Visa	(Recent addition/development) For remote workers earning income outside of SA.	Requires proof of employment outside of SA and minimum income.

Special Requirements for Children

South Africa has had stringent requirements for minors (children under 18) travelling into or out of the country, though these have been relaxed or modified over time. It is crucial to check the latest requirements, but historically, they include:

- An unabridged birth certificate showing the particulars of both parents.

- An affidavit of consent from the non-travelling parent(s) if the child is travelling with only one parent or with a non-parent.

Important Advice

1. **Always Check the Official List**: The list of visa-exempt countries is subject to change. Always check with the official South African Department of Home Affairs website or your nearest South African embassy/consulate.

2. **Yellow Fever**: A Yellow Fever vaccination certificate is required if you are traveling from or

transiting through a country that has a risk of Yellow Fever transmission.

South Africa has an extensive list of countries whose citizens are exempt from needing a visa for short tourist or business visits.

The length of the visa-free stay depends on the visitor's country of passport. The two main categories are 90 days and 30 days.

Visa-Exempt Countries for South Africa

1. Visa-Exempt for up to 90 Days

This group includes most of the European Union, the Americas, and key global partners.

Region	Countries (Non-Exhaustive List)
Europe	Andorra, Austria, Belgium, Czech Republic, Denmark, Finland, France, Germany, Greece, Iceland, Ireland, Italy, Liechtenstein, Luxembourg, Malta, Monaco, Netherlands, Norway, Portugal, Russian Federation, San Marino, Spain, Sweden, Switzerland, United Kingdom
Americas	Argentina, Brazil, Canada, Chile, Ecuador, Jamaica, Panama, Paraguay, United States of America, Uruguay, Venezuela
Oceania	Australia, New Zealand

Region	Countries (Non-Exhaustive List)
Asia & Middle East	Israel, Japan, Qatar, Saudi Arabia, Singapore, United Arab Emirates
Africa	Botswana, Ghana, Kenya, Namibia, Tanzania, Zimbabwe

2. Visa-Exempt for up to 30 Days

This group generally includes countries for shorter stays.

Region	Countries (Non-Exhaustive List)
Asia & Middle East	Hong Kong (SAR), Jordan, Macau (SAR), Malaysia, Maldives, South Korea, Thailand, Turkey
Africa	Angola, Benin, Cape Verde, Eswatini (Swaziland), Gabon, Lesotho, Malawi, Mauritius, Mozambique, Seychelles, Zambia
Americas & Caribbean	Antigua and Barbuda, Bahamas, Barbados, Belize, Bolivia, Costa Rica, Guyana, Peru

Important Notes

- **Annual Limit**: For some countries (like Angola, Namibia, Seychelles, Tanzania, and Zambia), the 90-day visa-free stay is limited to 90 days per calendar year.

- **Passport Requirements**: All visitors must have a passport that is valid for at least 30 days after their intended date of departure from South Africa and contains at least two unused blank pages for entry and exit stamps.

- **Purpose:** The visa-free entry is typically for tourism, visiting family/friends, and limited business purposes. If the purpose of the trip is for work, study, or to reside in South Africa for longer than the exempt period, a proper visa must be applied for in advance.

- **Disclaimer**: Visa regulations change frequently. Always confirm the latest requirements with the nearest South African High Commission, Embassy, or Consulate before booking your travel.

Chapter 23 — Pictures of South Africa

Photographs often capture what words struggle to express — the vast landscapes, everyday moments, and small details that define life in South Africa. These images offer a window into the country's diversity, from busy city streets to quiet rural scenes, from coastline to mountains. They also reflect the lived experience behind this book: places visited, roads traveled, and sights that leave a lasting impression.

This chapter presents a selection of photographs that help tell South Africa's story in a visual and immediate way.

23. Pictures of South Africa

Slightly North of Durban

Harrismith Bergville – if going to the Drakensburg, this is the town you come to and then head up to the Drakensburg.

North of Durban

Luthuli Museum near Durban

The Luthuli Museum is located at the former home of Chief Albert Luthuli in Groutville, KwaDukuza, South Africa. It is dedicated to preserving and sharing the legacy of the anti-apartheid activist and first African recipient of the Nobel Peace Prize.

Luthuli Museum

Rhodes University, Grahamstown

Rhodes University is a public research university located in Makhanda (formerly Grahamstown) in the Eastern Cape province of South Africa. Established in 1904, it is the province's oldest university and has a strong reputation for academic excellence, high postgraduate success rates, and the best research output per academic staff member in the country.

Steve Biko Museum

The Steve Biko Museum is part of the Steve Biko Centre in Ginsberg, a township outside King William's Town (Qonce), South Africa. The center is dedicated to preserving the legacy of Steve Biko, an anti-apartheid activist and founder of the Black Consciousness Movement.

Transkei refers to a former self-governing homeland and Bantustan in South Africa, recognized as a single, non-contiguous territory for the Xhosa people, which was granted nominal independence in 1976 but was not recognized internationally. It is now a region of the Eastern Cape province of South Africa and is also known as the Wild Coast, a popular tourist destination characterized by its rugged coastline.

Historical context: Transkei was a key part of South Africa's apartheid policy, designed to segregate the Xhosa population into a semi-autonomous region. Abolishment: It was officially reincorporated into South Africa in 1994 following the end of apartheid.

Modern-day geography: Today, the region is a picturesque coastal area known for its natural beauty and is a part of the Eastern Cape province.

Cultural significance: The area has historical significance and is the birthplace of Nelson Mandela.

Plettenberg Bay

The N2 highway runs through Knysna as part of the Garden Route along South Africa's southeastern coast. It enters the town after passing the Swartvlei Estuary and Sedgefield, offering scenic views as it winds toward the Knysna Estuary. This national route is a major artery from Cape Town towards KwaZulu-Natal.

Route details: *The N2 is a major national highway that goes through Knysna, a popular destination on the Garden Route.*

Scenic approach: *When approaching from the west, the N2 travels east from Sedgefield, crossing the Swartvlei Estuary and providing views of the landscape before entering Knysna.*

Major highway: *As one of South Africa's longest numbered routes, the N2 connects major cities along the coast, including George, Gqeberha (Port Elizabeth), and Durban, before continuing inland.*

Knysna Heads — the dramatic gateway between the lagoon and the Indian Ocean.

Port Elizabeth — Fishing

*Swimming at Port Elizabeth's rocky shoreline —
capturing a typical summer day on South Africa's coast.*

Youth kayaking along South Africa's scenic coast.

Tsitsikamma Khoisan Village, Garden Route

The Tsitsikamma Khoisan Village is a cultural and accommodation site located in the Tsitsikamma region of South Africa's Eastern Cape, near the Bloukrans Bridge. It aims to revitalize and share the history and culture of the indigenous Khoisan people while offering various lodging and adventure tourism facilities.

Overview of the Experience

Cultural Focus: The village offers visitors a chance to learn about the history and heritage of the Khoi-Khoi people. The aim is to create awareness and provide education on their traditional way of life, including the opportunity to see and stay in traditional Khoi huts.

Plettenberg Bay
© Tracy Springorum, used with permission

Plettenberg Bay, affectionately known as "Plett," is a picturesque coastal town located along South Africa's famous Garden Route in the Western Cape province. It is renowned for its stunning natural beauty, including pristine white-sand beaches, lush indigenous forests, and dramatic cliffs.

Plettenberg Bay
© Tracy Springorum, used with permission

Key Attractions and Activities

Beaches: Plettenberg Bay boasts several Blue Flag beaches, such as Central Beach, Lookout Beach, and Robberg Beach, which are ideal for swimming, surfing, and long walks.

Robberg Nature Reserve: This rocky peninsula is a provincial heritage site and offers spectacular hiking trails with stunning ocean views, a large Cape fur seal colony, and opportunities for land-based whale and dolphin watching. The Nelson Bay Cave within the reserve has yielded Middle Stone Age *artifacts over 100,000 years old.*

Wildlife Encounters: The area is a hotspot for marine life. Visitors can take boat tours for dolphin and whale watching (humpback whales migrate past between July and December, Bryde's whales are year-round residents). Nearby attractions also include Birds of Eden, the world's largest free-flight aviary, and Monkeyland Primate Sanctuary.

Outdoor Adventures: The diverse landscape of mountains, rivers, and ocean provides a perfect setting for a variety of activities, including sea kayaking, canyoning, abseiling, mountain biking, and trail running.

Keurbooms River Nature Reserve: This tranquil reserve is ideal for boating, canoeing, fishing, and picnicking, with opportunities to explore a pristine forest environment.

Plett Winelands: The region has its own burgeoning winelands, with estates like Bramon Wine Estate and Bitou Vineyards offering wine tasting experiences amidst beautiful scenery.

Vibrant Atmosphere: The town has a relaxed, upmarket atmosphere with a main street featuring quaint shops, bookstores, and excellent restaurants. It becomes a very popular and bustling holiday spot during the summer months (November to March), particularly over the Christmas period.

Plettenberg Bay Camp Site which is still very busy. Some campsites have fallen into disrepair in South Africa but this one is well run, and still very busy.

Camping in South Africa offers a wide variety of experiences, from coastal and mountain camping to wildlife-focused stays in national parks like Kruger. You can find many campsites, including resorts with full facilities, adventure farms, and safari camps, often listed on directories like SA Campsites, LekkeR Kampplekke, and SafariNow. It is important to note that wild camping is generally illegal and can be risky, so it is best to book a site at a designated location.

Gordons Bay, Western Cape, South Africa
©Quentin Londt, used with permission

Location: A harbour town located in the Western Cape province, part of the City of Cape Town metropolitan municipality.

Activities: Known for its beaches, including Bikini Beach and Main Beach, and opportunities for sunbathing, swimming, and water activities.

Attractions: It's also famous for its spectacular sunsets over False Bay and is surrounded by the Helderberg mountains and vineyards.

Gordons Bay, Western Cape, South Africa
©Quentin Londt, used with permission

Ballito Bay, KwaZulu-Natal

Tugela River Mouth, near Durban

Tugela River Mouth — where the Tugela River meets the Indian Ocean.

Knysna Heads, Western Cape

The Knysna Heads are a pair of iconic, colossal sandstone cliffs that form a dramatic and historically treacherous entrance from the Indian Ocean into the calm Knysna Lagoon in the Western Cape of South Africa. They are a famous landmark along the renowned Garden Route.

The best places to visit in Knysna include the Knysna Heads, the Featherbed Nature Reserve, and the Knysna Waterfront, offering a mix of stunning scenery, nature, and local culture. Other highlights are the Knysna Lagoon for water activities, various nearby beaches like Brenton-on-Sea and Buffalo Bay, and Thesen Island.

For a wildlife experience, consider the nearby sanctuaries or a visit to the Knysna Elephant Park.

Driving through South Africa

From Port Elizabeth back to Bloemfontein

Melville Johannesburg — April 2025

Lesotho Mountains – called the "Mountain Kingdom"

Lesotho is a sovereign, landlocked kingdom in Southern Africa, entirely surrounded by South Africa. Known as the "Kingdom in the Sky" due to its mountainous terrain, it is the only independent state in the world that lies entirely above 1,000 meters in elevation. The capital and largest city is Maseru.

On the N3 from Johannesburg to Durban

Port Elizabeth

Port Elizabeth is a major seaport city in South Africa, located on the southeastern coast of the Eastern Cape province. Its official name was changed to Gqeberha in February 2021, though it is still widely referred to as Port Elizabeth or P.E. by locals.

One of the Highest Bungee Jumps in the World – Knysna Bloukrans Bridge Bungy is one of the world's highest commercial bungy jumping sites at 216 metres.

Chapter 24 — South African Literature

South Africa's literature reflects the complexity of its history and the diversity of its people. From resistance writing during apartheid to contemporary voices exploring identity, memory, and change, the country's authors have long used storytelling as a way to confront reality and imagine possibility. Their works offer insight into the nation's struggles and its spirit, revealing perspectives that are as varied as the landscapes themselves.

This chapter highlights some of the key contributions that have shaped South African writing and cultural life.

24. South African literature

South African literature is rich, diverse, and deeply impactful, reflecting the country's complex history, especially the struggle against and transition from apartheid.

Here is a list of famous and essential books about South Africa, spanning autobiography, classic fiction, and contemporary works.

Editor's Note: Some titles appear in more than one list in this chapter. This is intentional, as certain South African works are both foundational classics and influential across multiple literary categories.

Essential and Iconic Works

Book Title	Author	Genre & Key Theme
Long Walk to Freedom	Nelson Mandela	Autobiography. The definitive account of Mandela's life, his struggle against apartheid, his 27 years in prison, and his role in building a new democratic nation.
Cry, the Beloved Country	Alan Paton	Classic Fiction. A powerful and poignant 1948 novel exploring racial injustice, the breakdown of tribal society, and the search for hope, told through the story of a Zulu pastor searching for his son in Johannesburg.

Book Title	Author	Genre & Key Theme
Born a Crime: Stories from a South African Childhood	Trevor Noah	Memoir/Humour. An accessible and often hilarious look at growing up as the child of a Black Xhosa mother and a White Swiss father during the final years of apartheid, when their relationship was a crime.
Disgrace	J. M. Coetzee	Modern Fiction. The 1999 Booker Prize winner (by a Nobel Laureate) is a stark and controversial novel examining the difficulties of life in post-apartheid South Africa, particularly themes of land, race, and sexual violence.
The Power of One	Bryce Courtenay	Historical Fiction. A moving coming-of-age story of an English boy named Peekay growing up in South Africa in the 1930s and 40s, using boxing to bridge racial divides in the lead-up to apartheid.

Book Title	Author	Genre & Key Theme
July's People	Nadine Gordimer	Classic Fiction. The Nobel Laureate's novel imagines a dystopian future where South Africa is plunged into a civil war, forcing a liberal white family to seek refuge with their former Black servant in his remote village.
Country of My Skull	Antjie Krog	Non-Fiction/Reportage. A deeply personal and poetic account by a journalist covering the Truth and Reconciliation Commission (TRC), exploring themes of collective guilt, memory, and the struggle for forgiveness in the new South Africa.

Other Highly Recommended South African Authors and Titles

- Zakes Mda — *The Heart of Redness* (2000)
  <u>Theme</u>: A post-apartheid novel exploring politics, history, and cultural identity.

- Zakes Mda — *Ways of Dying* (1995)
  <u>Theme</u>: Follows Toloki, a professional mourner, depicting life during South Africa's transition to democracy.

- Damon Galgut — *The Promise* (2021)
  <u>Theme</u>: Booker Prize–winning novel chronicling a white family across four decades of South African history.

- Mark Mathabane — *Kaffir Boy* (1986)
  <u>Theme</u>: A searing memoir about growing up in the apartheid township of Alexandra.

- Olive Schreiner — *The Story of an African Farm* (1883)
  <u>Theme</u>: A pioneering 19th-century novel, early feminist literature.

- André Brink — *A Dry White Season* (1979)
  <u>Theme</u>: A white schoolteacher risks everything to expose the death of a Black activist.

Here is a list of famous and highly-regarded South African fiction books, categorized to help you choose what interests you most:

THE CLASSICS: DEFINING SOUTH AFRICAN LITERATURE

These books are essential for understanding the country's literary foundation, heavily influenced by the apartheid era.

- Alan Paton — *Cry, the Beloved Country* (1948)
  <u>Theme</u>: A Zulu pastor travels to Johannesburg to find his son, highlighting racial inequality and urbanization.

- J. M. Coetzee — *Disgrace* (1999)
  <u>Theme</u>: Nobel Laureate/Booker Prize Winner. A controversial novel exploring justice, shame, and dignity in post-apartheid South Africa.

- Nadine Gordimer — *July's People* (1981)
  <u>Theme</u>: Nobel Laureate. Imagines civil conflict where a white family must seek refuge from their long-time Black servant.

- André Brink — *A Dry White Season* (1979)
  <u>Theme</u>: A politically awakening schoolteacher investigates a Black activist's death.

South African writers excel in modern, often gritty, genre fiction, reflecting contemporary social issues.

- Damon Galgut — *The Promise* (2021)
  Theme: A sweeping saga capturing South Africa's transition through a broken promise involving a Black domestic worker.

- Lauren Beukes — *Zoo City* (2010)
  Theme: Speculative fiction set in an alternate Johannesburg where criminals carry animal familiars.

- Deon Meyer — *The Dark Flood* (Benny Griessel Series)
  Theme: Crime thrillers exploring corruption, policing, and post-apartheid tensions.

- Mohale Mashigo — *The Yearning* (2016)
  Theme: Literary fiction blended with African spirituality; a woman returns to her ancestral roots.

- John van de Ruit — *Spud* (2005)
  Theme: A comedic coming-of-age novel set in a 1990s South African boarding school.

Wilbur Smith was a prolific author whose career was defined by sweeping adventure stories set across the African continent, with a significant number focusing specifically on South Africa and its turbulent history.

His primary works about South Africa are found within the epic Courtney Family Saga, which traces the lives of multiple generations from the 17th to the 20th century.

Here are the most famous and essential fiction books by Wilbur Smith centered on South Africa:

THE COURTNEY SERIES (SOUTH AFRICAN FOCUS)

The core South African experience is detailed through the lives of the Courtney family, particularly the Sean Courtney sequence and the Burning Shore sequence, which cover the colonial era, the Boer Wars, and the tumultuous 20th century.

1. Sean Courtney Sequence (1860s to 1920s)

This trilogy is generally considered the foundation of his work and is heavily set in South Africa, from the gold rush to the aftermath of WWI.

- *When the Lion Feeds* (1964): The saga's first book, following twin brothers Sean and Garrick Courtney as they come of age. It covers the Anglo-Zulu War and

the discovery of gold at the Witwatersrand
(Johannesburg).

- *The Sound of Thunder* (1966): Chronicles Sean
  Courtney's experiences during the Second Boer War
  (1899–1902) and its immediate aftermath.

- *A Sparrow Falls* (1977): Concludes Sean's story, set
  against the backdrop of post-WWI South Africa,
  including the Rand Rebellion (1922 miners' strike) in
  Johannesburg.

2. Centaine and Shasa Courtney Sequence (1917 to 1960s)

This group of books deals with a later generation,
focusing on the development of modern South Africa
and the rise of apartheid.

- *The Burning Shore* (1985): Follows Centaine de Thiry
  after her ship is torpedoed off the coast of South-West
  Africa (Namibia) during WWI, ultimately bringing her
  to South Africa to join the Courtney family.

- *Power of the Sword* (1986): Follows Centaine's twin
  sons, Shasa and Manfred, and their struggles against
  the political backdrop of the 1930s, leading up to the
  National Party's victory and the establishment of
  Apartheid in 1948.

- *Rage* (1987): Set in the 1950s and 1960s, this novel
  directly addresses the height of the Apartheid era,
  including the Sharpeville massacre, a pivotal event in
  South African history.

Standalone Novel

- *Gold Mine* (1970): An adventure thriller set in contemporary South Africa (1960s), focusing on the high-stakes world of the gold mining industry near Johannesburg.

Key Themes: Smith's South African novels are known for combining historical events with elements of adventure, romance, and conflict, often focusing on themes of:

- The search for gold and diamonds

- Colonialism and the exploitation of the land

- The tensions between the English settlers, the Afrikaans Boers, and the various indigenous Black groups.

Chapter 25 — The Other Side of South Africa

Every country has another side — the parts visitors rarely see, and residents learn to navigate with time. South Africa is no different. Beyond its beauty and cultural richness lie challenges that affect daily life: uneven public services, economic pressures, and social issues that stem from a difficult past. Acknowledging these realities is not about pessimism, but about understanding the country in full.

This chapter offers a level-headed look at the less visible aspects of South Africa, providing context for anyone considering life here.

25. The Other Side of South Africa

The negative narratives often overshadow the truly remarkable qualities of the nation.

The "other side of South Africa" is a story of extraordinary natural beauty, resilient institutions, deep cultural diversity, and vibrant human hospitality.

Here are the key areas that often get overlooked by international headlines:

Unparalleled Natural Heritage & Conservation

South Africa is one of the world's most "megadiverse" countries, ranking among the top for its richness in species and ecosystems.

- **The World's Floras in One Country**: It is home to the Cape Floral Region, the smallest but richest of the world's six floral kingdoms—and the only one to be contained entirely within a single country. This area, primarily around the Western Cape, holds an astonishing diversity of plant life, much of which is found nowhere else on earth (known as *fynbos*).

- **A Sanctuary for Wildlife**: South Africa is globally renowned for its conservation efforts.

    - **Kruger National Park** is an African icon, offering a world-class safari experience and is crucial in protecting the "Big Five" (lion, leopard, rhino, elephant, and buffalo), alongside hundreds of other species.

    - **The country is home to a vast network of South African National Parks (SANParks)**, including the rugged Drakensberg Mountains, the coastal wonders of the Garden Route, and the dense elephant populations of Addo Elephant National Park.

- **Breathtaking Landscapes**: From the spectacular Blyde River Canyon (one of the largest canyons in the world) to the iconic flat-top of Table Mountain and the meeting of the Atlantic and Indian Oceans at the tip of the continent, the sheer geographical variety is astounding.

The "Rainbow Nation" in Full Colour

Archbishop Desmond Tutu coined the term "Rainbow Nation" to celebrate the unity of South Africa's many cultures post-Apartheid, and this diversity is the nation's most profound human asset.

- **Twelve Official Languages:** The country recognizes twelve official languages (including Zulu, Xhosa, Afrikaans, English, and Sotho languages and South African Sign Language), reflecting a deep cultural mosaic. This means a traveler can experience a wide range of traditions, food, and music without ever leaving the country.

- **Music and Arts Innovation:** South Africa is a global powerhouse of musical innovation, giving the world unique genres like Kwaito, Amapiano, and vibrant strains of African Jazz and gospel. The contemporary art scene, particularly in cities like Cape Town and Johannesburg, is dynamic and internationally celebrated.

- **Exceptional Hospitality**: Despite its history and socio-economic struggles, South Africans are known for their warmth, resilience, and willingness to share. Tourists often recount stories of profound human connection and generous hospitality, particularly when engaging with local communities.

A rainbow over the South African landscape — a fitting image for a nation often described as the "Rainbow Nation."

Strong Institutions and Global Leadership

Beneath the political turbulence often reported, there is a foundation of robust democratic institutions and global influence.

- **Constitutional Democracy**: South Africa maintains a liberal democracy with regular, free and fair elections. Crucially, it has one of the world's most lauded constitutions, which champions human rights, equality, and dignity for all.

- **Independent Judiciary:** The country boasts a powerful and independent judiciary that has repeatedly ruled against the Executive branch, proving its strength as a check on political power—a vital sign of a functioning democracy.

- **Economic Hub**: South Africa is the most industrialized economy in Africa, with sophisticated infrastructure, a world-class financial sector, and a deep pool of academic talent. It remains a key strategic player and a gateway to the rest of the continent.

By focusing on these often-omitted features—the beauty, the people, and the institutional resilience—one begins to appreciate the full, complex, and beautiful reality of South Africa.

Chapter 26 — Banking in South Africa

Banking in South Africa is generally efficient and modern, with a system that is easy to use once you understand the main institutions and requirements. From everyday transactions to opening accounts and managing online banking, most processes are straightforward — though they may differ slightly from those in Europe or North America. Knowing what documents are needed and how the major banks operate helps newcomers settle in with confidence.

This chapter provides a simple guide to navigating the country's banking landscape.

26.Banks in South Africa

In South Africa, the cheapest options are generally found in the digital-only banks and the entry-level/pay-as-you-use (PAYU) accounts offered by the major traditional banks.

Based on recent reports on 2025 bank charges, here is a comparison of the most affordable options across different banking profiles:

Cheapest Bank by User Profile (2025 Analysis)

The winner changes depending on how many transactions you make, and whether you prefer an app-only bank or a traditional bank with branches.

User Profile	Banking Needs	Top 3 Cheapest Accounts (Approx. Monthly Cost)
1. Digital-Only/App Banking	Zero branch visits, high use of digital transfers/swipes.	1. TymeBank (Cheapest overall) 2. Bank Zero (Often free monthly fee) 3. Capitec (Strong digital focus)
2. Entry-Level/Low-Transaction	Basic banking, a few transactions (12–17 per month).	1. Absa Transact Account (Cheapest entry-level account) 2. FNB Easy PAYU

User Profile	Banking Needs	Top 3 Cheapest Accounts (Approx. Monthly Cost)
		(Highly competitive, low monthly fee) 3. Capitec Global One
3. Mid-Level/High-Transaction	High number of transactions, some cash withdrawals, debit orders (25+ per month).	1. Capitec Global One (Cheapest based purely on cost) 2. Nedbank MiGoals 3. FNB Easy Bundle

***Note**: The costs provided in bank reports are calculated using a fixed "basket" of common transactions (e.g., 4 debit orders, 4 card swipes, 2 cash deposits, etc.). Your actual cost may vary.*

Detailed Look at the Top Contenders

1. Capitec Global One

Capitec is often cited as a benchmark for affordability, especially for mid-level users. Their model focuses on transparency and low fees for electronic transactions.

- **Key Fees (Example)**: Monthly fee is around R7.50. Payments to other SA banks are R2.00.

- **The Advantage**: Very low fees for electronic transfers and payments. They also pay interest on positive balances in the transaction account.

- **The Caveat**: ATM cash withdrawals are charged per R1,000 withdrawn, which can be costly if you use ATMs frequently.

2. Absa Transact Account

This account is specifically designed for low-income or entry-level customers and has recently been named the cheapest in the low-transaction category among traditional banks.

- **The Advantage**: Has an extremely low monthly fee and often includes free features like counter cash withdrawals at retail partners.

3. TymeBank & Bank Zero (Digital-Only)

These banks have virtually zero or very low monthly admin fees and charge for specific, less-frequent transactions (like certain cash deposits/withdrawals or instant payments).

- **The Advantage**: If you use your card mostly for swiping (free) and do all transfers online, these are often the cheapest overall.

- **The Caveat**: They have very limited or no physical branch presence, which is a major factor for some users.

How to Get the Absolute Cheapest Banking

1. **Go Digital:** Always use the bank's app or online platform for payments, as these are significantly cheaper (often free) than doing transactions in a branch.

2. **Withdraw at Tills:** Instead of using an ATM, withdraw cash when paying for goods at major retailers (like Pick n Pay, Checkers, or Spar). This fee is usually much lower (often R2.00 or less) than an ATM withdrawal.

3. **Choose the Right Package**: Don't automatically go for the cheapest package. If you make 30 transactions a month, a bundled account with a higher fee but lots of free transactions might be cheaper than a PAYU account where every transaction is charged individually.

Capitec Bank

It has no deposit on site – instead done outside at ATM and there is a deposit fee. You can also get a sim card and a phone number and Internet connection from the bank which has partnered with a cell phone provider.

Chapter 27 — B-BBEE and Employment Equity

Broad-Based Black Economic Empowerment (B-BBEE) and Employment Equity are central to South Africa's efforts to address the inequalities created during the apartheid era. These policies aim to expand opportunities in business, education, and employment for groups who were historically excluded. While their goals are widely recognized, the practical implementation can be complex and, at times, debated by employers and citizens alike.

This chapter offers a straightforward look at how B-BBEE and Employment Equity operate in practice, and what they mean for people living and working in South Africa today.

27. B-BBEE and Employment Equity

South Africa's post-apartheid redress policies, specifically the definition of "Black people" under key legislation designed to address historical racial inequality.

Certain Chinese South Africans have more rights, or rather, more *access to opportunities and benefits*, than White South Africans under current legislation.

This difference in rights stems entirely from the legal definition used for affirmative action and economic empowerment policies.

The Key Distinction: B-BBEE and Employment Equity

The entire legal difference comes down to the Broad-Based Black Economic Empowerment (B-BBEE) Act and the Employment Equity (EE) Act. These laws are designed to redress the economic and employment injustices caused by apartheid.

1. Chinese South Africans (Qualifying Citizens)

In 2008, the Pretoria High Court ruled in the case of the Chinese Association of South Africa (CASA) that South African citizens of Chinese descent should be included in the definition of "Black people" for the purposes of B-BBEE and the Employment Equity Act.

The criteria for inclusion is strict:

- **Who Qualifies?** Chinese people who are citizens of South Africa and who were historically disadvantaged under apartheid. This specifically refers to those who:

  - Are citizens by birth or descent.

  - Became citizens by naturalisation before 27 April 1994 (the date of the first democratic election).

  - Became citizens on or after 27 April 1994 and would have been entitled to acquire citizenship by naturalisation prior to that date.

- **The Result:** Qualifying Chinese South African citizens are officially categorized as part of the "previously disadvantaged" group (alongside Africans, Coloureds, and Indians). This grants them access to preferential benefits such as:

  - **B-BBEE Ownership**: Counting toward "Black" ownership requirements for companies seeking government contracts or licenses.

  - **Employment Equity**: Being designated for preferential hiring and promotion under workplace quotas designed to reflect the country's demographics.

2. White South Africans

Under the B-BBEE Act and the Employment Equity Act, White South Africans are explicitly excluded from the definition of "Black people" and are therefore not beneficiaries of the preferential benefits, ownership, or hiring targets established by this legislation.

Conclusion

The legal framework of post-apartheid South Africa is built on correcting past racial imbalances.

Group	Constitutional Rights	Rights under B-BBEE/Employment Equity
White South Africans	Full and equal constitutional rights.	Excluded from preferential access to economic benefits and employment targets.
Qualifying Chinese South Africans	Full and equal constitutional rights.	Included as beneficiaries of preferential access to economic benefits and employment targets.

Therefore, in terms of economic redress and affirmative action, qualifying Chinese South Africans possess a legal status that affords them access to benefits and opportunities that are deliberately not available to White South Africans.

Broad-Based Black Economic Empowerment (B-BBEE or simply BEE)

Broad-Based Black Economic Empowerment (B-BBEE or simply BEE) is a fundamental and often complex policy implemented by the South African government to redress the economic inequalities and exclusion created by the apartheid system.

It is essentially a strategy for economic transformation aimed at increasing the participation of historically disadvantaged South Africans—specifically Black people—in the country's economy.

The Core Objective

The main objective of B-BBEE is to ensure that a substantial change occurs in the racial composition of ownership, management, and skills across all sectors of the South African economy.

The term "Black people" for the purpose of B-BBEE is defined as African, Coloured, and Indian (and, since 2008, qualifying Chinese people) who are citizens of South Africa. This excludes White South Africans, who are not considered historically disadvantaged under this legislation.

How B-BBEE Works: The Scorecard

B-BBEE is measured using a Scorecard based on five main elements (or "pillars") that companies must comply with to achieve a good B-BBEE status (or Level). The company's level is determined by the total points it scores out of 100+ points.

Element	Focus	Key Actions to Earn Points
1. Ownership	Measuring the level of Black ownership in the company.	Selling equity or shares to Black individuals, Black-owned trusts, or employee schemes.
2. Management Control	Measuring the representation of Black people in management and on the Board of Directors.	Appointing Black individuals to executive, senior, and junior management roles.

Element	Focus	Key Actions to Earn Points
3. Skills Development	Investing in education, training, and learnerships for Black employees and the unemployed.	Funding accredited training programs, learnerships, and providing bursaries.
4. Enterprise & Supplier Development (ESD)	Promoting supplier diversity and supporting Black-owned businesses.	Procuring goods and services from verified B-BBEE suppliers and providing funding/mentorship to small, Black-owned businesses.
5. Socio-Economic Development (SED)	Contributing to public benefit programs that benefit Black communities.	Donating to approved charities or public programs focused on education, health, or poverty alleviation.

Why Compliance Matters (The Incentive)

B-BBEE compliance is not technically compulsory for private businesses, but the market structure creates a massive incentive to comply.

- **Government Contracts**: Public sector tenders and contracts are almost exclusively awarded based on a combination of price and B-BBEE level. A high B-BBEE level is often mandatory to qualify.

- **Licensing and Concessions**: Many regulated industries (like mining, telecommunications, and finance) require a specific minimum B-BBEE status to obtain or renew operating licenses.

- **Preferential Procurement**: Large private sector companies are motivated to procure from businesses with a good B-BBEE score to boost their own Scorecard rating.

In short, a strong B-BBEE rating is considered a license to do business with the government and with major corporations in South Africa.

28 Disclaimer

The information provided in this book is for
informational and educational purposes only.
It is not intended as a substitute for consulting with a
qualified professional (such as a financial planner,
lawyer, or therapist) for your specific individual needs.
The author and publisher specifically disclaim any
liability for any loss or risk, personal or otherwise,
which is incurred as a consequence, directly or
indirectly, of the use and application of any of the
contents of this book. Your results may vary.

Martin Leigh in East London, South Africa, 2017